WHY
THE BEACH BOYS
MATTER

T0087718

M
M Music
Matters

Evelyn McDonnell

Loyola Marymount University

Series Editor

WHY THE BEACH BOYS MATTER

Tom Smucker

UNIVERSITY OF TEXAS PRESS
AUSTIN

Copyright © 2018 by Tom Smucker

All rights reserved

Printed in the United States of America

First edition, 2018

Requests for permission to reproduce material from this work should be sent to:

    Permissions

    University of Texas Press

    P.O. Box 7819

    Austin, TX 78713-7819

    utpress.utexas.edu/rp-form

♾ The paper used in this book meets the minimum requirements of ANSI/NISO Z39.48-1992 (R1997) (Permanence of Paper).

Library of Congress Cataloging-in-Publication Data available upon request

ISBN 978-1-4773-1872-0 (cloth: alk. paper)

ISBN 978-1-4773-1876-8 (library e-book)

ISBN 978-1-4773-1874-4 (nonlibrary e-book)

doi:10.7560/318720

For Sarah and Aaron

....

CONTENTS

....

WHY
THE BEACH BOYS
MATTER

Introduction

....

Of all the white American pop groups that hit the charts before the Beatles, only the Beach Boys continued to thrive throughout the British Invasion and then survive into the 1970s and beyond. No other white group embodied both sides of that split more-than-a-decade era we broadly call the Sixties, with their early surf, car, and summer pop and their later hippie, troubled, and ambitious rock. No other group can claim the Ronettes and the Four Seasons as early 1960s rivals; the Mamas and the Papas and Crosby, Stills & Nash as late 1960s rivals; and the Beatles and the Temptations as decade-spanning counterparts. The Beach Boys' battered but resilient history travels through the entire time frame of baby boomer dominance, from 1961's "Surfer Girl" through the decades-delayed release of *Smile* in 2004, to 2014's *Love and Mercy* biopic, and to Brian Wilson's excellent 2015 solo CD *No Pier Pressure*. Never *the* story of a generation, the Beach Boys' saga survives as one of a few that remain at a generation's core.

At the heart of the group were three brothers and a cousin from the lower-middle-class suburbs of Los Angeles. The Wilsons lived in Hawthorne in a modest two-bedroom home. Murry Wilson, the father, who sold industrial lathes, once got a song he wrote played on the air by Lawrence Welk. But Brian, the eldest brother, obviously was and is the Beach Boys' musical genius, able to decipher and recreate the vocal harmonies he heard on records by the time he was twelve years old. Dennis, the middle brother, was the sex symbol, drummer, troublemaker, and actual surfer who befriended Charles Manson in the late '60s, revealed a surprising songwriting talent in the '70s, and died an alcohol- and drug-fueled rock-and-roll death in 1983. Only age fourteen when the group began, Carl, the youngest brother, mastered the Chuck Berry and surf guitar licks crucial to their early sound, and proved to be the quiet brother who held the group together musically until he died of lung cancer in 1998. Mike Love, a cousin from nearby Baldwin Hills, sang lead on the group's first hits, wrote lyrics with Brian for many of their early songs, and served as the raconteur front man at their concerts. The Wilsons' neighbor, David Marks, as young as Carl, played on the group's early recordings and appears on those album covers. He replaced—and then was replaced by—Brian's high school and college buddy Al Jardine. When Brian quit touring in 1965, Bruce Johnston, a surfer and pop music insider, replaced Brian in the touring group, singing on the studio recordings beginning with "California Girls."

The group hit locally with their first recording, "Surfin'," was quickly signed by Capitol Records, and poured out a remarkable run of hit singles and albums from 1962 to 1965. After Brian's 1966 studio composing and recording masterpiece *Pet Sounds* failed to match the success of his earlier material in the United States, he abandoned his hyped and anticipated follow-up, *Smile*, and began a slow withdrawal from the group that would lead to his infamous three years in bed and eventual treatment under the control of the unscrupulous, manipulative psychotherapist Dr. Eugene Landy.

Falling out of fashion in America while remaining popular in Europe, Great Britain, and Japan in the late '60s, the group continued to tour without Brian, releasing a run of commercially unsuccessful but worthwhile material with and without his participation. By the early '70s, they had reestablished their hip credentials on record with the *Surf's Up* and *Holland* albums, as well as their tight, career-spanning concerts and renewed praise in the rock press; and they had added two members from South Africa, Ricky Fataar and Blondie Chaplin, during 1972–1973. In 1974, the group's early '60s hits were repackaged and reissued in the States on the *Endless Summer* double album and topped the charts for months, swelling their live audiences and overshadowing their newer music. As they coasted through the '80s as a glorified oldies band, it seemed there would be no new chapters to their story. But freed from Dr. Landy and remarried in 1995, Brian began touring with his own band, and in 2004 he completed, performed, and released *Smile*. In 2012, the surviving members of the original group—Brian, Mike, Al, Bruce, and David—temporarily reunited for a 50th anniversary tour and a new CD, *That's Why God Made the Radio*.

As I write, Brian tours with Al, Blondie, and the first-rate backing band that helped rehabilitate *Smile*. Mike controls the rights to tour as the Beach Boys, and includes Bruce in his also excellent, if less ambitious, band.

A complex net of contractual barriers and obligations remain as one legacy of the group's long history. In the '70s, they left Capitol Records for Reprise and then later signed with CBS. From 1970 to 1986, they co-released their material on their own label, Brother Records, in partnership with the three different major labels over the years. In time, Capitol gained the rights to the group's entire back catalog, permitting the creation of career-spanning retrospective boxed sets, anthologies, and re-issues. Brother Records is currently owed by Brian, Mike, Al, Bruce, and the estate of Carl Wilson, and leases the Beach Boys name to Mike's touring group. Brian's solo albums have been released by Sire, Nonesuch, Brimel, Giant, Disney, Capitol, and Rhino. Mike's 2017 solo CD was released on BMG.

I grew up in and around Chicago and have lived in New York City since 1967. I've traveled like many other pilgrims to the locations of the Beach Boys' California origins in the South Bay, as well as to the abandoned dance hall in Minnesota where they first glimpsed their national impact. My dad grew up in a small town in northwestern Ohio, just up the interstate from Lima, the childhood home of Beach Boy Al Jardine. My mom is from Newton, Kansas, a twenty-minute drive from Hutchinson, where the father of Brian, Carl, and Dennis Wilson and the mother of Mike Love were born. And yes, I am one of those sensitive old white men whose go-to-when-you're-feeling-blue album is still *Pet Sounds*. But I don't believe that makes it everybody's go-to album, and I do believe it's more likely that The Greatest Album Ever might have been recorded by Aretha Franklin, P-Funk, Miles Davis, Howlin' Wolf, or Kendrick Lamar.

I see Los Angeles as the urban blueprint for the last half of the US twentieth century, as New York City was for the first half. I view the Beach Boys as talented teenagers who could have been singing in the postwar lower-middle-class white suburbs of Chicago or Philadelphia. But because they were singing in Hawthorne, California, they had access to the details of commonly shared early '60s suburban teenage life alongside the rich, multiracial heritage of West Coast doo-wop, the electrified inventions of surf music, Chuck Berry on the radio, the Four Freshmen in the record store, and the LA recording studio as it matured into an artistic and technical counterpart to the Hollywood movie studio.

I don't hear those early car, surf, and summer songs as shallow yet charming time capsules. I hear them as fully realized music, naïve and profound, that will last as long as (maybe just white) people drive cars to work, school, and the beach, listen to recorded music, and live in detached single-family housing —or wish they could. I take the songs' innocence as the only way at that time to describe and explore a soon-to-be-dominant way of life that was supposed to have no significance at all, one that ironic sophisticates were expected to overlook or dismiss. I hear that innocence as open and honest enough to express the anxiety and isolation hiding inside the exuberance and pleasure.

Nor do I hear the Beach Boys' late '60s and early '70s music as failed attempts to out-hip the Beatles. I hear the music as an honest reflection of the bewilderment, opportunity, and dangers inside the struggle to stay relevant as the group's audience and culture changed, and as they negotiated the burden and the blessing of their pre-Beatles cultural heft. Then I hear that innocence disoriented and exhausted, even curdled into willful ignorance in the '80s, and slowly rehabilitated, now mixed with regret, when Brian broke free in the '90s and began touring again. It's a career that over the decades sometimes sounded exhausted, or no longer very significant, and then surprised with new bursts of creativity and cultural relevance.

Over these fifty-plus years, chronologies and biographies have been written and rewritten, narratives established, unresolvable disputes explored. New memoirs emerge, and new coffee table books plop down. But there has been no book that takes an honest look at the themes running through the Beach Boys' art and career as a whole, where they sit inside our culture and politics, and why they can still grab our attention. That's this book.

Tom Smucker

1

Harmony and Discord

....

When the Beatles and the Rolling Stones arrived and guitar band rock began to understand itself as an art form with a history, it settled on an origin story about the fusion of blues and country music that emphasized individual performers with an individual voice and guitar. Hank Williams plus Muddy Waters equals Elvis, so to speak. True enough, but that tale downplayed the contributions of vocal groups like the Soul Stirrers, the Moonglows, the Kingston Trio, and the Temptations, and obscured the music that helped shape the Beach Boys.

By the time they invented themselves in 1961, the Beach Boys had absorbed a lot of ideas about vocals. But only one was required for their entrance into show biz: low-budget, nearly a cappella doo-wop. Their debut single "Surfin'," originally released on the local Candix label, stumbled into a gold mine: fusing the subculture of surfing to the boasts of the teenage crew, pack, or posse. A group sound for a group.

Seeking entrée to the expanding teenage market, record labels were looking for doo-wop voices similar to thirteen-year-old Frankie Lymon, who sang lead on the Teenagers' huge 1956 hit "Why Do Fools Fall in Love." This still applied and worked to the Beach Boys' advantage as the '60s began. They looked young and sang high, except for double-voiced Mike Love, the crucial bass-baritone grounding on their harmonies and a midrange, youthful, nasal Chuck Berry acolyte on lead.

Often evoked by images of singing groups on the street corners of New York City, doo-wop's roots ran deep out in LA as well. The Crows' "Gee" was recorded on the East Coast in 1953 but first hyped by the West Coast DJ Dick "Huggy Boy" Hugg in 1954, the same year when he broke the Penguins' "Earth Angel" out of LA's Fremont High. Both hits can be credited with signaling doo-wop's pop chart debut.[1] And white kids in Southern California were paying attention. Mike Love recalls listening with his cousin Brian Wilson, as teenagers late at night, to Huggy Boy and Johnny Otis.[2] Dean Torrance of Jan and Dean makes a similar point about the African American musical origins of their music.[3] When Brian finally completed and released *Smile* in 2004, "Gee" was quoted on the opening track.

"Surfin'" was a big enough regional hit to get the Beach Boys a contract with Capitol, a photo shoot at Paradise Cove, and their first LP, *Surfin' Safari*, released in the fall of 1962. That year, they picked up one last but crucial addition to their vocal repertoire: the over-the-top, from-the-first-note, vulgar, ecstatic, gender-bent power falsetto of Frankie Valli of the Four Seasons, whose "Sherry" sat well above "Surfin' Safari" on the 1962 charts.

The Four Seasons' unprecedented New Jersey mix of jazz vocals, doo-wop, and early '60s studio smarts cleared an opening for the Beach Boys to incorporate this important piece of the rock-and-roll puzzle into their own group harmony sound. You can hear them borrow from, acknowledge, and challenge the Four Seasons on the *Surfer Girl* album's "Surfer's Rule."

The Jersey Boys respond on the flip side of "Dawn" with "No Surfin' Today."[4]

Without exposure to "Sherry," the Beach Boys had risked vocal harmony entrapment in the well-behaved world of white groups like the Four Preps. Absorbing lessons learned from Frankie Valli's example, they gained access to an entire culture stretching through the sacred-sexual frictions of Maurice Williams and the Zodiacs on "Stay"; Claude Jeter of the Swan Silvertones, and the golden age of Black Gospel quartets; the biracial Pentecostal Christianity Elvis absorbed in Memphis (which, as it happens, had its origins in downtown LA circa 1906); and further back, the African traditions of spirit possession and the Anglo traditions of rowdy industrial working-class Methodist worship.[5] By 1964, the Beach Boys could signal rock ecstasy by reaching for their own version of a power falsetto, most famously at the finale of "Fun Fun, Fun."

Inside this teenage vocal mix of crazy rock and sweet doo-wop, Brian Wilson was deploying an older generation's achievements to place his own voice and expand his group's harmonies. The pop jazz Four Freshmen from Columbus, Indiana,[6] with '50s hits like "It's a Blue World" and "Graduation Day," provided Brian a template for the inventive chord and key changes he refashioned to fulfill the emotional requirements of teenage doo-wop rather than the cerebral ones of collegiate mid-'50s jazz.[7] White group vocal pop jazz valued displays of virtuosity just like, if not as often as, bebop. By the time the Freshmen get to the word "blue" on their first big hit, you know you are far from the world of barbershop quartets. Just as important, the Four Freshmen's high tenor Bob Flanigan modeled a way for Brian to sing high at the top while still inside the group harmonies some of the time, and high at the top of his range in a sweet falsetto when he sang lead.

The Freshmen were a self-contained quartet live, playing brass, bass, and drums while they sang, prefiguring the Beatles era live rock band lineup, while emulating earlier big band vocal ensembles like Mel Torme's Mel-Tones, where women sang high as "Velvet Fog" Torme oozed out from the middle. Flanigan took the woman's part, and when appropriate, made it the lead. But unlike their smooth modern harmony predecessors, the self-contained Freshmen sang hard; Flanigan compared them to a brass section. That aggression, the high tenor lead, the inventive harmonies, and the ability to pivot into sentiment and nostalgia were all access points where Brian Wilson could pull Freshmen approaches into doo-wop, into rock and roll, into rock.

On one level, this allowed Brian to stretch the boundaries of four-chord pop music, with complex harmonies providing the flow. For one great example, open any Beach Boys songbook for guitar or ukulele and check out the chord changes in "The Warmth of the Sun."[8] On another level, Brian's bebop-tinged doo-wop opened up a space for emotionally direct, yet emotionally multilayered vocals, as in "Warmth of the Sun." Since Brian usually collaborated with plainspoken lyricists like Mike Love, Gary Usher, Roger Christian, and Tony Asher, the complexity was musical, not verbal. The music had to reveal yet contain the isolation and the comradery, the fun and the sorrow, the security and the anxiety, the eternal and the commonplace.

Unlike the Four Freshmen, or post-doo-wop groups like the Temptations and Four Seasons, who held very different voices at the top and the bottom of the harmonies, the Beach Boys were four or five voices similar in range and timbre, and for the formative years, genetically linked—three brothers, a cousin, and a friend. They were more like the Everly Brothers, magnified by Brian's early and continuing deployment of double tracking on the vocals, highlighting the more-than-the-sum-of-its-parts phenomenon of overtones, notes created and heard but not sung by close voices in harmony. All this brotherly virtuosity gave Brian's studio productions with the Beach Boys a depth unavailable to his musical idol, Phil Spector. Brian was producing *and* writing *and* singing. He was Phil Spector *and* Ronnie Spector *and* the Ronettes. While Spector was the masculine mastermind of his pop compressed extravaganzas, and Brian was often equally domineering while recording, Brian was also identifying with and appropriating girl group vocals, attitudes, and frequently subject matter. The supplicant, insecure boyfriend of the idealized girlfriend was edging out the cocky, one-of-the-gang surfer and car buff. Or mixing the two on songs like "Don't Worry Baby."

But if this group wasn't always singing about being a group, what did those harmonies mean? Sometimes they were a part of the palette, a piece of the orchestration, a technique used to underscore or highlight a phrase. And sometimes, for the Beach Boys, the give-and-take between solo, duet, and five-part harmony could articulate the tension between, support for, and interdependence of the individual and the group. This is a great theme in Beach Boys music and biography, with the group itself a shifting and frequently unstable mix of crew, friends, family, spouses, artistic collaborators, and business partners. It's the ultimate tension between Brian Wilson and the Beach Boys.

That interdependence of individual and group can also be

turned inside out in their music: the individual as a collection of parts; the individual struggling against disintegration or leaning into integration and full expression; the individual holding it all together or letting it all hang out. Was it Don or Phil Everly, and if you didn't listen closely, John or Paul? Which one of the Mills Brothers? Which Marvelette? Which Wilson brother?

Maybe all those subtly different voices were only one Beach Boy, one I-contain-multitudes Wilson. Maybe *Pet Sounds* really was a solo album, as some have claimed, even if, or maybe because Carl and Al, as well as Brian, took solos. Maybe the harmonies not only expressed but created the cohesion of the group and served the same functions for the individuals inside the group. If so, there's one more pot of glue provided in those harmonies to hold the individual and the group and the music together: the possibility of transcendence and grace, love and mercy.

Bios and memoirs mention Sunday mornings and weekly choir rehearsals at the Inglewood Covenant Church (Wilson family) and Wednesday youth nights at the Angeles Mesa Presbyterian Church (the Loves), and note that Sunday morning was a Murry Wilson–free musical influence: Dad didn't attend.[9] But that's about it. There's almost no mention of the churches' music, and Google can't even locate an Inglewood Covenant Church. Ross Barbour begins his Four Freshmen memoir by recalling how great the four-part harmony sounded on "The Doxology" before family dinners after church on Sundays in Indiana.[10] So I'm going to assume, given the recorded evidence, the largely Lutheran family histories, and Brian's rapport with Freshmen harmonies, that the music at the Love and Wilson churches was midcentury, Euro-American, mainline Protestant hymnody.

"The Lord's Prayer" was the flip side of the Beach Boys' 1964 "Little Saint Nick" but didn't appear on an album until an Australian '80s rarities LP. It's the classic Albert Hay Malotte tune with the classic King James lyrics sung sincerely, with Beach Boys harmonic flourish that deepens rather than distances the piety. The only straight-ahead Christian song they would ever release, unless you count "We Three Kings,"[11] it's hidden on a flip side as if to say, "This is what we come out of, but it's not where we're going." Maybe they needed to throw out the bathwater of midcentury mainline religious convention to save the baby of rock-and-roll sanctification. Maybe Capitol considered it a mid-'60s risk. Yet "The Lord's Prayer" remains one of their vocal high points.

There are other nods to Protestant hymnody in the Beach Boys' music. The wordless, a cappella "Our Prayer" was originally intended to open and provide a coda for 1967's abandoned *Smile*, as it did when Brian and his crew finally completed *Smile* in 2004. As a leftover track from those original sessions, the song was first released on the Beach Boys 20/20 album in 1969, one reason that hodge-podge collection shouldn't have held together but did. A "Lord's Prayer" minus lyrics, "Our Prayer" foregrounded the pieces of doo-woppish, Freshmenish, Christianish, Inglewood Covenant Church choir Brian had been using since 1963.

"In the Parkin' Lot," from 1964, like "The Lord's Prayer," begins and ends with a slower a capella chorus that frames the rocking middle. Some may hear this as a composition by the boy genius who had too many musical ideas for too few song topics. I hear it as a spiritual frame around a smaller secular moment

—the minutes before school starts when you're making out with your girlfriend in your car, a gift of cosmic dignity for not-so-special kids at a not-so-special high school in a not-so-special suburb. And by implication, that cosmic dignity is extended to the music's creators and consumers as well. It's the same mystery Brian tapped into on *Pet Sounds*: overtones that, as reported by Brian and Carl, added a level of spirituality to a record that would have sounded peevish or self-pitying without it.[12] On songs and albums that could end as dramas about groups or individuals at odds with themselves, harmony offered a higher level of resolution.

Too easily skipped over, those vocal harmonies could be dismissed as inauthentic, even repressive, especially in the early '60s. The individual voice was breaking free, from Presley to Baez to Dylan to Cooke. Folkies turned rockers unfamiliar with pop jazz vocal traditions unfairly dismissed the Four Freshmen's influence on the Beach Boys as corny and shallow, even hopelessly square. But Brian was fashioning complex harmonies on top of his complex chord changes inside pop songs that could pull you in deep. That's why the harmonies still worked in concert even when group members were feuding in later years—they contained those dramas of conflict and resolution inside the vocals themselves. And that's why the harmonies didn't work when they were used on uninspired late-career songs as a musical trademark trying to recover the lost world (and sales) of the early '60s—that wasn't their function.

Sometimes the harmonies were well intentioned but weren't a good fit. Brian's 1988 "Love and Mercy" single off his first solo album was originally released with a wordless choral finale that overpowered this modest, heartfelt gem, even though it matched the subject matter. The movie of the same name wisely rolls the credits with a stripped-down live version that drops that choral ending, maintaining the movie's interpersonal focus. The only time I've heard the whole song work together was at the end of the Brian Wilson tribute at Radio City Music Hall in 2001, where Brian himself sang "Love and Mercy," followed by a full-strength finale by the entire Boys Choir of Harlem, an appropriately big wrap for a very big evening.

And yet and yet and yet. The Beach Boys 50th anniversary CD, *That's Why God Made the Radio*, opens with a miniaturized "Our Prayer" and ends with a Brian Wilson trilogy and a final song, "Summer's Gone," situated inside wordless harmonies as perfect and appropriate for that album's autumnal vibe as anything on *Pet Sounds* or *Smile*. Framing their fifty-year history, Brian captures a very big soundscape, even if the songs in the middle of the album are easily ignored. The music's interplay of transcendent chorale and heartfelt solo vocals makes you wonder if Brian might still need the Beach Boys to reach his best lonesome, isolated stuff. Or a version of the Beach Boys. Or the idea of the Beach Boys. Or the gifts accessible inside their harmonies.

2

Cars and Guitars

....

In 1955, "Gee" and "Earth Angel" joined Chuck Berry's "May-bellene," Fats Domino's "Ain't That a Shame," and Bill Haley's "Rock Around the Clock" on the pop charts. Even with Little Richard and Elvis still on their way, rock and roll had arrived. In Fullerton, California, a short drive from the Beach Boys' hometown of Hawthorne, Fender Guitar was beginning production runs of the Stratocaster, for many the ultimate and still the best mass-produced solid body electric guitar, followed two years later by the first mass-produced electric bass guitar, the Precision. Out in Detroit, Ford unveiled the Thunderbird, and Chevy the Bel Air, as the entire Chrysler line got a design upgrade; and in Washington, DC, President Eisenhower wrangled with Congress over how to finance the construction of the interstate highway system. Car sales rose 37 percent in one year, vehicle production in the United States neared 10 million, unionized auto workers won a forty-hour work week and health benefits, and the percentage of employees in unions nationwide peaked at over a third. Historians dubbed it the Golden Age of the Car.[1]

Leo Fender was a farm boy when Fullerton was full of orange groves. An inventive tinkerer in the tradition of Thomas Edison and Henry Ford, he fooled around with radios as a kid, built custom PA systems, liked Hawaiian music and Western swing, and never learned how to play or even tune a guitar. But Fender listened to the needs of musicians looking for clear but louder guitars with sustain, and he tinkered into existence an instrument that permitted the creation of Dick Dale's surf music in nearby Balboa as well as much of the music that would come out of Bakersfield, Los Angeles, Chicago, Detroit, Nashville, and beyond.

Dick Dale says that he could not have become King of the Surf Guitar without Leo Fender's creation of the Stratocaster and the Showman Amp.[2] The spread of Fender guitars spawned lots of instrumental combos far from Dick Dale and his Deltones: the Ventures in Seattle, the Trashmen in Minnesota, the Shadows in the UK, the Atlantics in Australia. Some groups said they played surf music and some said they did not, but after the Beach Boys fused doo-wop to surfing in 1961 and needed to flesh out a live set, there was a close-at-hand guitar-based surfing sound in formation for them to borrow from and promote. By the time the Beach Boys released *Surfin' USA* in March 1963, their second and most guitar-centric LP ever, Brian's kid brother Carl Wilson and their next-door neighbor David Marks could whiz though Dick Dale's instrumentals "Let's Go Trippin'" and "Misirlou" onstage and in the studio, along with some crucial Chuck Berry licks.

Those licks counted, because the "Surfin' USA" hit single, which was Berry's "Sweet Little Sixteen" refashioned with surf-centric lyrics and guitar tone, was Brian Wilson's first fully realized production. Mixing Berry-style wordplay with wordless harmonies inspired by the Four Freshmen, "Surfin' USA" carried Berry's signature guitar moves atop a driving, pulsating bottom that was less syncopated than Berry's. Jumping next to a romantic ballad, the Boys strung out the surf theme (along with their original Paradise Cove photo shoot) for a third and final go-round, September 1963's *Surfer Girl* LP and hit single.

Their fourth album, *Little Deuce Coupe*, repositioned the sound of the surf guitar back where Chuck Berry knew it belonged: inside their car songs. This didn't expose the fickle insincerity of pop; it revealed the obvious: if you weren't a surf purist, the car songs and the surf songs were the same. Both hot rods and surfboards were creations of and advertisements for a new world of affluence, industrial expertise, and youthful leisure taking shape most obviously in Southern California.[3] Not everybody could have an ocean, but lots of teenagers could have a car.

Like all great folk art, the musical combination of the Fender Stratocaster and Precision Bass imitated and elevated the world around it, where the fathers worked in aerospace plants, ran sheet metal shops, and sold metal lathes, and their sons heard the mechanical yet beautiful rhythms of a gearshift motor cruising 'round the town. This wasn't pop jazz about migrating across the country on "Route 66" with Nat King Cole—that was a hip idealization of the baby boomers' parents' journey. This was new music about cars, not as a source of transportation, but as the site of teenage dreams, a ride that like surfing had become its own destination.

While this music was evolving out west, boom times for the American auto also helped birth an analogous new musical combination of technology and talent in Detroit that elevated automotive assembly-line collaboration, and announced the arrival of the Great Migration of African Americans from south to north at the controls of the recording studio: the Motown sound. In that car-centric city, its engineers and producers were paying close attention to the car radio, made commonplace by the invention of the transistor and replacement of the bulky, fragile radio tube. That made the car the first location of an audience's exposure to new music, and first impressions were crucial. Motown would play potential hits through a tinny studio radio that mimicked the sound available to potential customers in an early '60s car until the studio producers found the right mix.[4] And in that mix, Motown's Funk Brothers house band nurtured pop music's first genius of the Fender Precision Bass, James Jamerson, author of the bottom line on "What's Going On," "My Guy," "Get Ready," "Baby Love," "Heat Wave," "Road Runner," and hundreds more. His bebop creativity inside a Top 40 pocket anchored the music with a depth and sparkle that would pull it through a dashboard listen into your ears, into the dance floor, and into the home hi-fi. Aspiring bassists of what became the British Invasion raved about "the guy who plays bass on Motown," before record album liner notes recognized instrumentalists by name.[5]

From the beginning, the Beach Boys were creating car songs alongside the surf songs. "409" (the engine size of a V-8 Chevy in 1962) was the flip side of the "Surfin' Safari" single and the last track on side one of the same named album. "Shut Down" and "Little Deuce Coupe" were also car-song flip sides on hit surf singles and tracks on those early surf-themed albums. The *Little Deuce Coupe* LP gathered up these flip sides with some new car-themed songs. You can hear it as quickie bet-hedging from Capitol Records that the surf fad was fading and it was time to repackage. I hear it as a tour de force trip to the New Frontier's troubled heart.

"Ballad of Ole' Betsy," the second track, a bittersweet love song to a car, requires some historical context. Deuce Coupe is specifically a 1932 Ford, cheap and therefore popular in the '60s for customization—John Milner's hot rod in *American Graffiti*. Ole' Betsy is an early prewar Dodge or any old car. Old Betsy was the name of "King of the Wild Frontier" Davy Crockett's rifle in real life and in legend for the 1955 hit Disney TV series, Technicolor movie, and song. And so, while "Little Deuce Coupe" is another wonderful bragging-about-my-car song, "Ballad of Ole' Betsy" is something different, an apprehensive-about-love-coming-to-an-end song, with the love object a rusting piece of machinery that echoes the talismanic gun in a childhood fairy tale about western expansion and taming the wilderness. Sung without irony or distance, "Betsy" is framed by a soaring yet tense, wordless falsetto introduction and a reverential vocal harmony conclusion. Cornball white male emotional disconnection to some, or maybe merely incongruous WTF. But for me, "Betsy" is an audaciously honest departure from the guitar-based car songs, an uncovering of the mysterious affections and anxieties generated by the Golden Age of the Car, potent enough to get revived live in concert by the current touring Beach Boys led by Mike Love.

"Spirit of America," the second track on side two, hymns the 1963 land speed record set by Craig Breedlove in a jet-powered car as an essentially strange victory, highlighting the Christlike incarnation and journey of the car's jet engine from a plane in the heavens to the earthbound Bonneville Salt Flats raceway. Here the wordless falsetto, the lyrics, and the singing maintain a tension between fear and awe, as if there is something both spiritually terrifying and spiritually rewarding about the whole attempt.

Tom Smucker

The rest of the album's material is less striking but hardly filler—a religious, romantic, mechanical, emotional, social, and artistic portrait of early '60s car culture, all on one album. With the confidence gained from this achievement, the Beach Boys were ready to create a masterful three-car-song summation on side one of 1964's *Shut Down Volume 2*, their fifth album.[6]

The lead track, "Fun, Fun, Fun," opens with Carl Wilson's guitar homage to "Johnny B. Goode" and "Roll Over Beethoven," and lives up to its promise by jumping into the cleverest wordplay of Mike Love's career in a story-line call with a chugga-chugga response, as if the singer and the car are sharing the narration. As the song builds, celebrating a young woman who sneaks out in her father's Thunderbird to drive like an ace with the radio blasting, the background vocal harmonies shift between commentary and chorale, the instrumentation oscillates between Berry quotes and surf guitar bottom; and it all resolves, as the father takes his car back and the daughter goes off with the singer, into the soaring falsetto conclusion that still draws a standing ovation when either Brian or Mike closes his show with it. Ecstasy attained in a gently gender-bending two-minute anecdote from a hamburger stand.[7]

The second track is the sublime "Don't Worry Baby," a multilayered vocal exploration of male anxiety and mortal fear resolved by female empathy and Eros. In this song, let's just notice for now that the car in this drama is both the site and the source of the anxiety, not a means of escape or any kind of solution. "In the Parkin' Lot," mentioned earlier, follows immediately with its transcendent harmony frame, and takes place inside a parked car. But despite its title and the front-cover photo, the rest of the album contains only one other car song. The next song on side one is the classic and carless "The Warmth of the Sun," completed after the assassination of John F. Kennedy.[8] Here's that four-song progression: Fun, Worry, Parked, Sun.

The follow-up album, *All Summer Long*, has a couple of car songs, but summer has now replaced surfing and cars as the master concept. Brian Wilson's compositions and production are now moving away from their Fender guitar center. The rocker David Marks is replaced by the returning folkie Al Jardine, a better fit vocally. "California Girls" finds the group no longer portrayed as neighborhood buddies cruising 'round the town, but as rock stars who have been all around this great big world, summed up in the song's grand intro, and who are yearning for home—to the clippity-clop rhythm of a cowboy movie. "Barbara Ann," the last hit single before *Pet Sounds*, is an updated acoustic salute to doo-wop roots.

As the Beach Boys were spending less quality time in their cars, the cars themselves were less inspiring. Automatic transmissions and windows-up air conditioning broke the link between the sound of chord changes and gears shifting. President Kennedy was gunned down riding in a Lincoln convertible, Ralph Nader touched a nerve about car safety, and the public started noticing smog. Fifty years later, what is the music to be made from driving a Prius? A Chevy Volt? A Subaru?

Some overviews of the Beach Boys' career hear the recordings just before *Pet Sounds* as an advance toward sophisticated production and introspection, away from the earlier adolescent surf, car, and summer songs. That view underestimates the car songs, which are rooted in a metaphor and means of social organization complicated by the passage of time but still at the center of most American lives, and ever more central to lives in the rest of our rapidly industrializing, urbanizing, polluted world. It also ignores the wide net of emotions, perspectives, and musicality the Beach Boys spread across these songs, and the difficulties they would face finding other subjects as deeply aligned in their own daily habits with the daily habits of their audience.

Dismissed and then rediscovered by their fans, the car songs' popularity forced the later Beach Boys to negotiate the border between Golden Age of the Car nostalgia and reactionary ignorance. In 1974, after the massive success of the pre–*Pet Sounds* compilation *Endless Summer*, Capitol, anticipating the bicentennial (and arguably Reaganism), released a slapdash but best-selling followup, *Spirit of America*. That compilation repositioned the title song as simply patriotic, downplaying its anxious undercurrents and the larger reason the Beach Boys car songs outlasted the early '60s hot-rod genre—they could go deeper.

If there was an honest update of "Spirit of America," it wasn't a car song at all. It was the second verse of Carl Wilson's "The Trader" from 1973's *Holland* LP. At their deepest level, the Beach Boys car songs suggest that there might be something essentially strange about a civilization built around concrete highways and cars. "The Trader" takes that insight deeper yet, tracing back our mobility to the so-called settling of the continent by Europeans after their arrival by sea. The wordless background chorus kicks in to make the destruction sound not only ruthless but profoundly, even cosmically weird. And that would be about as far as anyone in the group or in the audience would want to take it.

Direct attempts for late-career car hits got caught on a still cruising snag: cars were no longer in the foreground of the band's daily experience, and more often were only in the foreground for the audience when they were an aggravation. Writing new car songs was almost like writing about indoor plumbing. You took it for granted except when it wasn't working. Car ads emphasized tranquility, prestige, and mastery as frequently as fun. Pop songs might reference a car as a status marker, not a hangout. Country music uses pickup trucks the way it once used tractors, as regional and subcultural signifiers. Toby Keith endorses Ford F-150s, and I've heard him mention trucks in his songs and show a video in concert featuring a pickup, but I've never heard him sing a song about or to a truck.

The famous cello triplets at the end of "Good Vibrations" were the updated, honest, one-step-removed homage to the chugga-chugga gearshift guitars of the past, recognition that the sounds were still inside our subconscious, but now buried deep. When Brian successfully wrote a song in which he's driving in his car (into the sunset) on "Pacific Coast Highway" (2012), he used a musical vocabulary developed after *Pet Sounds*, appropriate to the subject at hand: the passage of time, the end drawing near. The song does not draw our attention to the silent automatic transmission on his Cadillac, and how it allows him to contemplate mortality, at least not directly. He isn't thinking about or singing about his car, but he's still in his car.

Like the best early Beach Boys songs about romance, the early car songs could recapture the power of first falling in love, if given perspective. The milieu that first heard itself mirrored in "Shut Down" and "Don't Worry Baby" could grow into sentimental adults who appreciated the foundational music of our time and place, and sometimes we did. Or, as the twenty-first century ground through its second decade, regress into resentful old white men, stuck in unbearable traffic-jammed commutes, listening to talk radio crackpots.

3

Suburbs and Surf

....

As soon as there were big cities in the United States, there were suburbs, accessible by carriage, and then ferry boat and rail, offering commuters the domestic portion of Thomas Jefferson's dream: green grass, clean air, rural independence, and separation from the riffraff. But it took the introduction of Henry Ford's inexpensive, reliable Model As and Ts; the nationwide demand for paved, connected roadways; and the surge of 1950s postwar prosperity to flip suburbia from an enclave for the snobs into the mainstream of American life.[1]

In 1962, when the Beach Boys released "Surfin' Safari," California had surpassed New York in population, and Los Angeles was the pacesetter for other emerging suburbanized megalopolises like Houston and Atlanta and the expanding edges of older cities like Chicago and New York. The West Coast had the sunshine and the coastline and defense plant jobs and oil and crops and a solid tax base and good public roads and schools. The '50s had seen the African American population double in New York City; in LA the multiple was eight, as the civil rights movement pulled the South into the twentieth century. California's New-Deal-to-New-Frontier governor Pat Brown easily won a second term running against the former US vice president, failed presidential candidate, and California native Richard Nixon.

The catastrophic reckoning with white America's refusal to grapple with racialized economics was two years away. The anonymity of interstate beltways, sprawl, malls, fast-food chains, big-box stores, and abandoned main streets still lay in the future. The world the Beach Boys rose inside of, and sang out of, hit an intersection of rising expectations shared by small towns and small cities and the non-elite mass suburbs. The everyday details in "Fun, Fun, Fun" and "Be True to Your School" were as accurate in that moment for Hawthorne, California, as for Hutchinson, Kansas, and Lima, Ohio—and much of what lay in between. And as the Boys discovered when they started touring further from home, what they thought might be a regional limitation in their music was instead a crucial factor in their nationwide and even international popularity. Their first eye-opening, big-money gig occurred in Sacramento, a ninety-minute drive east from the Pacific Ocean. That same month, May 1963, the Boys filled a Minnesota dance hall with a capacity of seventeen hundred, and had to turn a thousand fans away.[2]

Why? Why not. They could sing, they could rock, they looked like their audience, they shared a new leisure youth culture gaining shape across a prosperous America, and they could crystalize that new culture with the new metaphor of surfing. They slung enough accurate slang and place names in their surfing songs to sound legit—and that mattered—without getting tagged as elitist insiders—and that mattered too.

By 1962, the surfer as a symbol was almost as elastic as its predecessor, the cowboy, encompassing *Gidget* movies as well as made-for-surfer documentaries like *Surfing Hollow Days*. Representing prosperity's new leisure, surfing could simply stand for lots of fun time at the beach. Or it could pull together a new complex of deeper meanings: an ecstatic, dangerous, fun-loving negotiation with nature at the West Coast conclusion of the conquest of the continent—white youth paddling out beyond the reach of puritanism, patriotism, and maybe straight, square life itself, and then surfing back to shore. Charmingly bogus or certifiably sincere, these currents would run through surf symbolism, including the beach party and spring break movies, the mainstream breakthrough of Bruce Brown's more-than-a-travelogue *The Endless Summer*, and the cultural ascent of the Beach Boys themselves.

Whether a mystical quest or just a chance to watch young men and women dance in swim trunks and bikinis, surf symbolism all shared the same SoCal knack for self-promotion and the early '60s desire (or obligation) to sum up the dreams and aspirations of midcentury mid-America, using whatever mass media were currently available. That's what the Beach Boys realized in Minnesota and inland Sacramento. Their audience was ready to be represented by their representation of life in Southern California. And with a little help from Chuck Berry, that's what the Boys were ready to give them. "Surfin' USA" and "California Girls" portrayed a welcoming cultural moment you could migrate to, or identify with from a distance. Midwest farmers' daughters and their boyfriends and kids in Sacramento and the characters in *American Graffiti* could move to LA or just attend a hometown concert and purchase a copy of *All Summer Long*.

Real surfers didn't really like the Beach Boys in the early '60s.

Brian Wilson never surfed, and while at first that seemed surprising, in the long run, this distance brought the Beach Boys closer to their audience, since it was a distance they usually shared. In fact, there was a period in the early '70s when the Beach Boys were more popular in the UK and New York City, where they could be admired as masters of important pop forms and abstractions, than in LA, where they could be dismissed as so-last-decade hometown cornballs. *Pet Sounds* received a warmer welcome across the Atlantic on debut in 1966; *Smile* was first performed in 2004 by Brian and his band at the Royal Albert Hall in London.

Real surfers also didn't like, or more accurately, flat-out loathed the early and mid-'60s beach party and spring break movies, where mainstays Annette Funicello and Frankie Avalon hung out in an imaginary Malibu about as close to actual surfing as a backyard swimming pool. And for a while, there was some real cultural energy generated in the space these movies inhabited between real life and real surfing. That's where Annette's *Mickey Mouse Club* fans and Frankie's *American Bandstand* fans, aging out of adolescence, could find confirmation for their aspirations to achieve the good life, as idealized on a fictional California coastline.

The Beach Boys, the Hollywood-hungry surf music pioneer Dick Dale, and the Brian Wilson collaborator Gary Usher all found employment in these movies. And therein lurked danger. The genre was an energetic but unstable mixture of an earlier Allen Freed–style rock-and-roll exploitation movie whose thin plot shuffled the romantic leads around a lot of music acts (Look, it's Chuck Berry! And there's the Moonglows!) fused to a Hollywood gimmick as old as Moses, featuring a lot of nearly nude cavorting that concluded with the reassuring restoration of monotheism or monogamy or modesty. *Rock, Rock, Rock!* meets *The Ten Commandments* at *Beach Blanket Bingo*.

This combination blew apart during the Vietnam War years —no movies about having fun and returning to a normal life for now. Soon, the model Chris Noel, who co-starred in *Beach Ball* (imaginary Malibu) with Edd "Kookie" Byrnes, and in *Girl Happy* (imaginary Fort Lauderdale) with Elvis himself, would visit veterans in a stateside hospital, sign on as an Armed Forces Radio DJ, and force a troop-requested format switch from pop jazz standards to lightly censored Top 40 ("We Gotta Get Out of This Place" and "Good Vibrations"; okay, no "Puff the Magic Dragon"). Noel toured Vietnam continually, suffered her own peacetime PTSD, and remains a critic of Jane Fonda and an advocate for Vietnam vets to the present.[3]

Applying a Chris Noel–style story about lighthearted parties ending with the war to the Beach Boys' career illustrates a partial truth. Yes, the Boys often signified the good times, and the war changed lives, including theirs. Like many of their fans (including me), Carl Wilson maneuvered with his draft board and flirted with some jail time. But the war years did not end the Beach Boys' career. The era complicated the image they projected, in the long run in a good way. To get there, they had to struggle, sometimes with the public and sometimes with themselves, to distinguish their own multilayered, conflicted music from beach party perkiness; and they still struggle. Promo blurbs for current touring remnants of the Beach Boys still hype their concerts as a momentary return to sunny California, and the concerts are that for sure. But they are also a return to a moody, lonely, strange and anxious California that was never a part of *Beach Ball* or *Girl Happy*.

Proving they could get serious, in a late '60s relevant—or some would say pretentious—fashion forced the Beach Boys to acknowledge those moody, lonely, strange, and anxious strands that were woven into their music from the beginning. Accessing that side of their experiences, personalities, and public image created a space to move into when the world of beach parties disappeared; and this left the Beach Boys' legacy that much richer.

Their biggest party-movie contribution, 1965's *Girls on the Beach*, foreshadows some of these contradictions. The movie opens with a title song featuring one of Brian's wordless choral intros, casting a vibe of heterosexual mystery across a long tracking shot of an apparently endless group of bikini-clad young women running in the sand. The lyrics promise that all the girls are in reach, and then add a qualifying "if," while a Wilsonian melodic wistfulness suggests the singer's continuing and possibly permanent distance as an observer. Later in the movie (a typical ass-shaking, cross-dressing, cleavage-revealing, virtue-restoring concoction), an uncomfortable-looking Brian moves on camera to sing his ode to hopeless love, "Lonely Sea," flipping the ocean metaphor from a fun location to a vortex of isolation. The only party moment comes when the group lip-synchs "Little Honda" back at the club.

Of course, the beach party format didn't care if you were lonesome Brian Wilson singing "Lonely Sea" or tragic loser Frankie Valli singing "Dawn" or proto-feminist Lesley Gore singing "Leave Me Alone." It would all get pleasantly forgotten as the plot wrapped up at the movie's end. When the war got hot and that format and its wrap-up blew away, it looked as if the Beach Boys might get sealed off in the first half of the '60s with Annette and Frankie. But they made the transition during the war years, thanks in part to some continuity acquired from developments in a different surf movie genre.

Throughout the late '50s and early '60s, surfer movie makers like Greg Noll and Bruce Brown filmed at California and Hawaii surfing hot spots, and then showed these documentaries in rented auditoriums to surfers with live narration and a recorded instrumental tape. In the '50s, Brown used Hermosa Beach Lighthouse jazzer Bud Shank for the music; as tastes changed, Brown switched to rock combos but rarely cranked up the hardcore surf guitar sounds. The movies were about riding waves, and also paddling out, hanging out, wiping out, and searching for those perfect waves, so the music needed to match up with the mellow and mysterious interludes as well as the dramatic highlights. After several two-year cycles of filming, editing, and then exhibiting and narrating his movies in person, Brown gambled on a documentary about an around-the-world search for waves by two California surfers. When his *The Endless Summer* debuted in 1964, it sold out so often on the surf movie circuit that Brown gambled again, added his narration and the music to a soundtrack, and in 1966 rented theaters in Wichita, Kansas, and then New York City to screen his epic and prove its appeal to audiences far from the South Bay. And far from the South Bay, Pauline Kael gave the movie a rave review in the *New Yorker*.

As *The Endless Summer* played to full houses at Manhattan's Kips Bay Theater, Brown turned down all the national promotion and distribution offers until he found one that would stick with the original illustration of a surfer and his board in silhouette against an enormous setting (or maybe rising) sun and not demand a new campaign featuring girls in bikinis.[4] His movie wasn't about bikinis; it was about a quest, a skill, a commitment to leisure that could be sort of spiritual. On the soundtrack, "Theme from The Endless Summer" by the Sandals set an appropriately wistful, questing mood, far from Frankie Avalon or Dick Dale.

This wasn't just artistic integrity—the bikini promo would have been a costly miscalculation. Bruce Brown knew what he was selling: *The Endless Summer* with the original illustration would go on to gross $30 million. And at its core, his film was closer to what the Beach Boys were selling than the beach party movie, although the band had been selling that as well. But it would take the Boys another eight years to puzzle out where they would next fit into the ongoing dance between surfing art and surfing commerce.

In the early '70s, working to prove their up-to-date counterculture credibility, the Beach Boys created an intuitive connection between the early idealizations of their surfing songs and the idealizations of their new, with-it, hip songs. The key was "Surf's Up," the ballyhooed centerpiece of *Smile*, brought out of the vaults, polished up by Carl, and placed at the conclusion of the 1971 *Surf's Up* album, which also included Carl's similarly melodic, shimmering, wordy "Feel Flows" and "Long Promised Road." None of these songs were directly about surfing; none of them updated the jargon from "Surfin' USA" or "Surf City." But they caught a mood and a perspective.

In 1972, the great second-era (short board) surf movie *Five Summer Stories* incorporated these new songs on the soundtrack, as well as Carl's "The Trader" and other cuts from the *Holland* album, some classics like "Good Vibrations," and their earliest hits including "Surfin'." The movie places itself as a surfing update, referencing the surfboard traffic jams and collisions on overcrowded waves, the war in Vietnam, the end of the draft, lame chamber of commerce surf contests, and, quite enthusiastically, the rise of female surfers. The Beach Boys had a history as well, and that proved a surprise match to the movie's surf history. Brian's revived finale, and Carl's three hippie poetical-political-spiritual cuts complement the wave-riding shots, updating the vibe of the Sandals' original "Theme from The Endless Summer." Carl's "Long Promised Road" is a particularly good fit, with a sequence of real surfers doing real surfing after and in spite of the intrusion of commercial hype. Both the song and the authentic surfing portray a spiritual quest.

I don't surf. I can barely swim. I don't follow the sport of surfing in the way I follow baseball and basketball. But I find something inexpressibly moving about watching Gerry Lopez surf in *Five Summer Stories*. It makes me wonder if the guy isn't onto something with his combination of surfing, snowboarding, yoga, and meditation. It makes me wonder if "Surfin' Safari" didn't indeed announce the beginning of a quest. Ten years after "Surfin'," the Beach Boys had finally, if accidentally, recorded music used in a real surf movie.

But during that ten-year transition, Vietnam was not the only blow to early '60s New Frontier optimism that the Beach Boys and their audience absorbed or deflected. Like the suburbs, and like white rock and roll, surfing had and has a racial subtext, or maybe it's an over-text. Surfing was a native Hawaiian cultural and spiritual practice adapted by Euro-Americans, and then Euro-Australians and then Euro–South Africans and then Europeans, with varying degrees of sensitivity. In *The Endless Summer*, and elsewhere over the following five decades, surfing's representations could drift into a good-natured, postcolonial, white imperialism of leisure. Although the Supremes (singing "Surfer Boy" by Holland Dozier Holland!), James Brown, and Stevie Wonder appeared in the party movies, there weren't any black, brown, or beige bodies in the swimsuits. The boundaries of racial segregation were shrinking, but that meant they had moved, not disappeared.

In June 1963, Governor Pat Brown won passage of the Rumford Fair Housing Act (FHA) in the California legislature; in his view, this was an obvious addition to the legacy of the civil rights movement and his reelection landslide mandate the previous year. In December 1964, that Fair Housing Act was overturned two to one in a statewide referendum, repealed by white majorities in every county except underpopulated far northeast Modoc.[5] In August 1965, Watts exploded. In November 1966, Ronald Reagan beat Brown in a small-government, property-rights, law-and-order landslide and served two terms as governor before becoming president.

Now California became the cutting edge of retrenchment. White America had agreed to dismantle the legal structure of Jim Crow in the South with the July 1964 Civil Rights Act, and to end racial disenfranchisement with the August 1965 Voting Rights Act. But from Boston to Detroit to Chicago to LA, white America balked at dismantling, or even acknowledging intentional, legally and governmentally imposed geographic racial segregation and its economic consequences. To simplify, here's one example: when the federal government began insuring home mortgages through the New Deal FHA, it disqualified (refused to insure) homes in African American and racially integrated neighborhoods. Blacks were legally blocked by federal policy from getting amortized mortgages into the '50s.[6] The postwar suburban expansion was racially segregated by law, as well as by custom.

In April 1968 Martin Luther King Jr., then laying the groundwork for the Poor People's Campaign the next month in Washington, DC, was assassinated in Memphis while mobilizing support for the African American sanitation workers' union recognition struggle. Both efforts exemplified what King called the second phase of the civil rights movement, the economic rights phase—a phase that still hasn't happened. He was gunned down at the Lorraine Motel, a Stax Records hangout, where Steve Cropper and Wilson Pickett had written "In the Midnight Hour." His killing felt almost inevitable, and that still feels unbearable. Nearly a quarter century later, in 1991, LA police were caught on camera beating Rodney King and were acquitted; and as in 1965, LA burned again.

In this social crisis, suburbs were identified as the destination of a white flight that left behind a shrinking tax base in what used to be called the inner city. Seen this way, suburbs weren't an extension linking rural and city life, but were legally imposed white garrisons for commuting racists who enforced terror in the ghettos and then supplied the candidates for juries that acquitted those terrorists when they were caught on videos. Over

Tom Smucker

time, California's best-in-the-nation statewide school system disintegrated as the statewide tax base shrank into balkanized islands of affluence and poverty. In reality, the entire nation legally desegregated but geographically resegregated education. At the minimum, it was obvious that good roads and cars and cheap gas weren't going to solve every social problem. That didn't make the idea of suburbs racist, but it sometimes made it tragic. It could have been, sometimes is, and can still be different. I know. I spent my '50s grade school years in an economically humble, multiracial western suburb of Chicago, a place that legally and financially could not have existed in previous decades in the United States.[7]

As the Beach Boys phased into the age of real-world home ownership, they were also becoming showbiz professionals, rock stars losing touch with the complications, woes, joys, compromises, and cultural markers of white, lower-middle-class suburbia. The eldest son, Brian, graduated from Hawthorne High before the group became the Beach Boys. The youngest son, Carl, had to transfer to Hollywood Professional High School once his teenage celebrity became a hassle magnet in the regular teenage world. That meant that the band's portrayal of one type of American average life could never evolve beyond the innocent and honest observations, dreams, and worries of Mike's and Brian's adolescence. Success prevented them from consciously or unconsciously confronting the legally imposed economic realities separating Watts from Hawthorne. At the same time, white suburbia itself transitioned into a sprawling, splintered, less idealized project, and spawned a variety of pop music identities and regionalisms as the migration to Los Angeles got replicated and modified in Houston and Atlanta, and became more and more pervasive across America.

The postwar mass suburbia that the Beach Boys once sang about was receding into a memory of a way of life that, in a fairer world, might have realized the multiracial optimism of the band's musical influences. Typically, and tragically, the same social forces that had created that new mass suburbia were incapable of untangling it from an intentional ignorance about America's original racial sin, an ignorance as old as Thomas Jefferson. And that failing would leave a lie inside Jefferson's pastoral ideal, and a lie or at best a lost hope inside the early '60s.

....

In 1972, I was settling into my career as a technician at what we used to call the Phone Company when I got a totally atypical call at work from the assistant to the choreographer Twyla Tharp, who was developing what would become a classic modern dance and ballet mash-up entitled *Deuce Coupe*. As Tharp conceived it, that mash-up would be danced to Beach Boys songs, only she couldn't get her hands on the group's old LPs. Her assistant had called the *Village Voice*, and they gave him my number. I was leaving on vacation and put them in touch with a fellow fan, Terry Morgan—as far as I knew, the only other person in New York City who owned every album the Beach Boys had released.

Terry loaned Tharp the records, and *Deuce Coupe* debuted in February 1973. Of the sixteen songs in the piece, more than half couldn't have been located without Terry's help. Some, like Dennis Wilson's "Cuddle Up," were from the Beach Boys' current albums. But Tharp had grown up in Rialto, California, where her parents ran a drive-in on Route 66. So obviously, she would re-member Beach Boys material predating *Pet Sounds*.[8]

At the time, Capitol Records was beginning to notice that the hits the label still controlled from the Beach Boys' back cata-log were rousing concert crowds, and not just at ballets. Some-one, probably Mike Love, brilliantly decided to title Capitol's 1974 pre–*Pet Sounds* anthology neither "Back to the Beach" nor "Beach Boys Great Hits" but *Endless Summer*, tying it to the movie and the quest and the mystery, the elusive and resilient symbol of surfing. And somebody brilliantly picked twenty songs that fit together, no ringers. And somebody brilliantly did *not* feature a model in a bikini on the cover, but hired Vietnam vet Keith McDonnell[9] to draw a gatefold illustration with the Beach Boys as grizzled old hippies poking out of Henri Rousseau–style return-to-nature foliage, with just a suggestion of John Rambo back from Nam hiding in the backwoods, as if to say, "We sur-vived, we exist, times changed, the vibe is intact, and our old stuff still rocks." This was not watching a beach party movie on late-night TV while maintaining an ironic distance. This was playing prewar Beach Boys after the war, after Watts, after Man-son, after Altamont, after Stonewall, after Janis, Jimi, and Jim had died, after *Surf's Up* and *Holland*, after Roe v. Wade, after the Sixties ended in 1973. But it wasn't as if these things had never happened. The country, the Beach Boys, and their audience had changed. Yet on the other side of that change, people were still living their average lives, or hoping to return to what they imag-ined average life could be, and that made the songs on *Endless Summer* more compelling. In their rediscovery, the songs repre-sented a potent recollection, reality, and dream of average life.

The album hit number one after four weeks and stayed on the charts for three years. In New York City, the Beach Boys went from playing an armory in the Bronx for an audience of one hundred, to Carnegie Hall, and to Madison Square Garden, where the response to the *Endless Summer* hits was so raucous that the concrete balconies started swaying. Those old songs weren't simply appreciated; they were *embraced* like prodigal sons returning home.

Or maybe *clung to*. The songs described a social reality that in 1974 may have felt more powerful because we were at the beginning of a long, but at the time unacknowledged, economic uncoupling. The shared prosperity that greeted boomer babies after World War II had peaked. Obscured by Watergate, the symptoms of the new era were noted but not absorbed: the oil shortages, the trade deficits, the supposedly impossible combination of inflation and unemployment.[10] Welcome to inequality. The beach party wasn't coming back. But if the endless summer had become an unlikely aspiration, it could remain a golden memory that old Beach Boys songs could render vivid and, in the listening, a destination.

That same year, hip label Warner Bros., home of the Beach Boys' up-to-date, popular, arty, hifalutin comeback albums, was also rereleasing vinyl twofers of their four wonderful, quirky, poor-selling, post–*Pet Sounds* albums, *Smiley Smile*, *Wild Honey*, *Friends*, and *20/20*, with cover art of a gal in a bikini under a palm tree. This image applied to precisely one song on all four albums: *20/20*'s excellent "Do It Again." When in doubt, default to the bikini. The *Smiley-Friends* double even featured an inside graphic of a woody station wagon, when those two albums

Tom Smucker

would have been more accurately represented by wind chimes, headphones, and a hash pipe. It would take another sixteen years, when twofers of the old vinyl albums were reissued on a single CD with the original artwork and insightful notes from the first and best Beach Boys biographer, David Leaf, to accurately repackage that late '60s music.

"Do It Again" would be the final Beach Boys song to successfully reference surfing as a physical endeavor as well as a metaphor. It was a modest hit in the States in 1968, and a bigger hit overseas, especially in the UK, not because everyone in London started surfing, but because the Brits could understand the use of the song's surfing metaphor to mark time's passage, the Beach Boys' passage through their own pop history, and our passage as their fans. Later attempts to do it again, again, to squeeze hits from similar material, did not succeed. The mystery was missing. The details weren't accessible. The Boys had grown too old to be able to portray faux teenagers.

Honorable mention must go to two later career appropriations of surf music classics first released in 1963. In 1977, Bruce Johnston's *Going Solo* LP scored with a disco version of the Chantays' "Pipeline," which did well enough to get its own twelve-inch bootleg remix.[11] In 1987, the Beach Boys collaborated with the Fat Boys and Dweezil Zappa on a Latin Rascals edited, hip-hop update of the Surfaris' "Wipe Out," on the soundtrack of the Fat Boys comedy *Disorderlies*, which also featured a brief cameo from the Beach Boys. It wasn't "Walk This Way," but Fat Boys meet Beach Boys is a moment that deserves recognition.

Although "Do It Again" would prove to be the group's last hit surfing song, Brian and Dennis continued to be drawn to the sea and coastline for inspiration. For Brian, that period runs from 1971's "'Til I Die" to 2012's "Pacific Coast Highway." In 1997, Dennis released a well-received, soulfully dramatic solo album, *Pacific Ocean Blue*, whose title cut referenced the Pacific tainted by the blood of slaughtered whales and otters. Neither Carl's two solo albums nor Mike's first one referenced surfing or the sea, and Carl's compositions never found that "Feel Flows" groove again.

Then, in 1988, the Beach Boys minus Brian scored a huge hit with "Kokomo," a convincing sun-and-fun update about escaping to an imaginary Caribbean island, with steel drums, an accordion, great hooks, their signature vocals, and a faint echo of *Pet Sounds'* "Sloop John B." Yes, it was featured in a stupid movie starring Tom Cruise as a bartender, and the video with aging Beach Boys as swinging fun seekers looked peculiar. But you could picture those old neighbors from Hawthorne, who still lived in a modest suburb and might be average fans like yourself, taking it slow on a vacation in Kokomo, and that was the song's great charm and achievement.

It was never duplicated. Instead, Mike Love soldiers on in his mid-'70s as a diehard horndog, working images of scantily clad young women into his live shows, most recently as cheerleaders in the onstage video accompanying "Be True to Your School." (Come on, Mike, that's weird, and not what the song is about.) At the same time, his current concerts successfully link surfing, the group's history, and environmental catastrophe on "Summer in Paradise," the title cut from the flop 1992 CD, performed live with an elaborate background video about dolphins, despoiled beaches, polluted oceans, clear-cut forests, and endangered sea turtles. His 2017 CD *Unleash the Love* references the environment on some of his new peace-and-love tunes, and revives "Do It Again." We shall see how all this plays out as Mike continues to position his version of the Beach Boys as America's Band, and America continues to elect officials who deny climate change and work to dismantle the Clean Water Act.

These days, surfing is a global hobby, literary obsession, sports career, counterculture and marketing gimmick, a slippery symbol of too many things and none at all. Southern California coastline real estate is now a domain of inflationary exclusivity, not mass affluence—nowhere for an average teenager in a tract home sneaking out at dawn to catch a wave. Skateboarding is the democratic, multiracial, international transformation surfing experienced when mass suburbia turned inland and embraced skateboarders as battered dancers on the urban ocean of the concrete sprawl, its sound a blend of hip-hop, punk, and metal. Beach Boys music that linked surf and suburbs in the '60s might have ended up sealed off into an idealized, inaccessible past. But as it turned out, that past would generate much of our post–World War II, baby boomer culture, including the Boys' own more than half-century career.

4

Studio and Stage

....

Along with the freeway, the fiberglass-foam surfboard, the Fender
Stratocaster, Top 40 radio, and the 45-rpm single, the march of
technological progress awaiting the creation of the Beach Boys included the spread of a network of recording studios that stretched
from low-budget neighborhood walk-ins to independents to LA's
own corporate answer to New York, Capitol Records. The Wilsons were not just a family that liked to sing around the piano.
Murry, the father, was an aspiring, occasionally successful song-
writer, familiar since the mid-1950s with the insides of the studios, especially Gold Star, where Brian would later watch and
learn from Phil Spector and record the bulk of *Pet Sounds* and
Sunflower.[1] For his sixteenth birthday, after he spent a year picking apart the harmonies on Four Freshmen records, Brian's parents gave him a two-track Wollensak tape recorder, and he started
experimenting with overdubbed vocals.[2]

Unlike the Beatles, the Temptations, and the Four Seasons, all initially bar and club bands, the Beach Boys formed
by recording "Surfin'" at World Pacific studio, releasing that
regional hit and signing with Capitol. And as the hits continued, Brian Wilson took control. By their second album, he was
producing the Beach Boys' music in his choice of studios with-

out getting the credit on the album. By the third album, Capitol expressed its thanks on the back cover: "to Beach Boy Brian Wilson for producing . . . the finest Beach Boys album yet." This quick ascent is usually attributed to Brian's drive and genius, but it's also the result of his family's familiarity with, interest in, and ability to navigate the world of studio recording.

By the early '60s, the accessible art form of recorded music was only about forty years old, and now it was everywhere. Thanks to the transistor, radios had shrunk in size, rendering both social and solitary listening mobile. You could hear "In My Room" alone in your room and "Fun, Fun, Fun" in your car with your friends. It would be decades before VCRs and videotapes, and then DVDs, smartphones, and streaming would make moving images equally portable. The only other cultural artifact at the time that could compete with musical recordings for accessibility, affordability, and variety was the written word, print on paper. And it took half a millennium to get from the Gutenberg Bible to the mass-market paperback. When the Beach Boys released *Surfin' Safari*, the 33⅓ long-playing album as a physical, commonly available, cultural product was only about a dozen years old. The recording studio itself was about twenty years old. The idea that the studio had created a new category of artist, the record producer—similar to the movie director as an "author" of a recording or a movie—was even newer.

By 1949, pivotal producer Mitch Miller was creating something different in the studio with belter Frankie Laine: post-swing, pre-rock pop with its own sonic textures. That's historically important: for today's ears, it was an approach that led to Bobby Darin's "Mack the Knife" and then a dead end, because it failed to use those new sonic textures to express enough emotional subjectivity. Not so for composers Jerry Leiber and Mike Stoller ("Searchin'," "Jailhouse Rock," "There Goes My Baby"), who moved themselves into the studio by the late '50s. Controlling the recording, they could realize the sound and feel that they had imagined when they composed their songs, demanding credit on their records not only as writers but as producers.

Others were recording music conceived as its own art form, like Frank Sinatra's *In the Wee Small Hours* in 1955 or Rodgers and Hammerstein's *South Pacific* soundtrack in 1958. But these recordings relied on writers who wrote songs, arrangers who arranged them, singers who sang them, and producers who produced the records. Leiber and Stoller were composing recordings as recordings. They were Rodgers and Hammerstein, Alfred Newman, Kenneth Darby, and Joshua Logan combined. They were Rodgers and Hart and Nelson Riddle.

Leiber and Stoller's protégé Phil Spector pushed this to the next step, making the producing and the producer (himself) the center of his Wall of Sound hits. With his flamboyant personality and LA accessibility, Spector was the creative role model for Brian. At Motown, Berry Gordy realized something grander as an uber-producer, heading a studio with an identifiable sound during the Detroit years, across his factory of singers, musicians, composers, and producers. The boss with the last word, he was often the source of the final mix. The Kingston Trio, the Beach Boys' predecessors at Capitol Records, were a less obvious influence; they entered the studio as the '50s gave way to the '60s, overdubbing group vocals on multiple takes, miking each trio member separately, adding presence and depth[3]—strategies the

Tom Smucker

Boys would borrow for their own vocals, along with the Trio's striped shirts.

And then along came Brian Wilson in his early twenties, able to hear all the voices in a harmony vocal and imagine a recording as a multilayered composition before entering the studio. Once the Beach Boys had teamed up with Jan and Dean in concert, and Jan had shown Brian around the studio and suggested he use the studio musicians who came to be known as the Wrecking Crew, all the pieces were in place. Not because the Wrecking Crew had a sound. They weren't Motown's Funk Brothers; they weren't James Brown's JBs. The Wrecking Crew were a shifting collection of rock-era LA studio pros—Hal Blaine and Earl Palmer on drums, Carol Kaye and Ray Pohlman on bass, Leon Russell on keyboard, Glen Campbell and Tommy Tedesco on guitars—who could and did play any kind of Sixties pop, and who moved from patronization to admiration for Brian's musical gifts. The Hal Blaine character's "You're a genius" pep talk to Brian in the *Love and Mercy* movie during the *Pet Sounds* sessions sounds accurate, if not in every specific. YouTube will cough up videos of Carol Kaye, sometimes with Brian, raving about his jazz-influenced bass lines.

So Brian Wilson could come into the studio knowing how he wanted the instrumental backing track to sound; and they could record it, layer on layer, exactly the way he imagined, after enough takes. Then he knew how he wanted the vocal solos and harmonies to sound, and the Beach Boys could sing it, exactly the way he imagined, after enough takes. And when it all fit together, it sounded just as Brian had imagined it all.

This was the natural next step after Mitch Miller, beyond

Spector and Leiber and Stoller, a step back from Gordy. This made the studio the instrument for a personal statement, for singing and writing and producing the songs. And that would feel important when rock-era fans wanted to claim our own history and found we could trace the sound of the Beach Boys back to their very first recordings. It's why those earliest Beach Boys albums still sell and why *Pet Sounds* can feel not like a break, but like a culmination. It's why the four-CD *Pet Sounds Sessions*, originally released in 1997, is still selling digitally, allowing us to hear that album as it was recorded, layer on layer. The Beach Boys weren't a group discovered by a record producer; they discovered themselves in the studio.

That doesn't make their music better than records created by multiple collaborators, or sung a capella. But it does mean those studio albums can be considered personal statements, just like Bob Dylan's earliest recordings of his own songs in his own voice accompanied only by his own guitar. The studio, including the Wrecking Crew, was Brian's guitar.

Nonetheless, the Beach Boys also had to figure out how to present themselves and their music onstage, and a live performance is a different pop art form than a studio recording. In storytelling about their history, one famous key moment comes when Brian decides to quit live performances and stay in the studio while the rest of the group continues on tour, returning from the road to add the vocals for *Pet Sounds*. This is accurate and poignant given the friendship and family dynamics, but not unusual for mid-'60s division of pop music labor. Brian frequently opted out of performing before settling in for *Pet Sounds*, and Beach Boys counterparts the Temptations and Four Seasons were also out touring while instrumental tracks were being re-corded by studio pros, Wrecking Crew counterparts, in Detroit or New York City. All three groups might get back to the studio, record their vocals on the top, work out how to perform the new music live, and go out on the road again. Advances in studio re-cording made this possible and useful. Only the Beatles, once they had obtained Super Fame status, could get away with skip-ping live performance entirely—or maybe had to for their own safety.

Books and movies about the Temptations acknowledge this give-and-take, and describe both studio and stage as sites of cre-ation. This balance is hard to avoid; the Tempts were famous for their choreography in concert, while the larger mechanism of Motown itself, including the studio, is always understood as a participant in their story.

Once the Beatles had taken over the American Top 10 and the British Invasion was under way in 1964, of the American acts, only the Four Seasons along with the Beach Boys and Mo-town continued to survive and thrive at the top of the charts. All three had mastered the art of producing multilayered pop hits with impact by 1964. All three continued to sound fresh on their recordings, and even fresher once they had heard the Beatles and George Martin. All three had a web of self-aware musicians, writers, and studio savants who understood what the self-aware Brits were up to. All three could impress on the road and cre-ate in the studio, and if you narrow down the focus at Motown to the Temptations, all three had a group vocal sound that was identifiable live and on record.

The *Love and Mercy* movie does a great job—the best I've

ever seen in a movie—of showing a pop artist (Brian) working in the studio with his engineers and musicians, using real musicians hired for the movie to portray the real musicians of the Wrecking Crew at work in the studio. But because this is a Brian bio, it doesn't focus on the other members of the Beach Boys when they're out on a tour, so it leaves the impression that little thought was given to the concerts. Yet it was up to the live, in-person Beach Boys to personify the changes and continuities across the group's tumultuous first decade, to figure out in the mid-'60s how to work "God Only Knows" and "Good Vibrations" into a live concert along with "Fun, Fun, Fun," and how to portray onstage the discoveries made in the studio.

Today, a half century after traveling from *Surfin'* to *Pet Sounds*, the '60s studio along with all the musicians in it could be poured into a laptop, and a kid improvising on a laptop could get a turn at the neighborhood band shell or rec center, plugged into the amps and the speakers alongside the guitar band, jazz combo, salsero, and emcee. That places *Pet Sounds* or *All Summer Long* or *The Beach Boys Today!* near the halfway point in a progression of what one book calls *The Producer as Composer*.[4] When Brian seizes control for the *Surfer Girl* LP, that's a link on a chain leading from Thomas Edison inventing the phonograph in 1877 to sample-based hip-hop and electronic dance music. This is pop music history as the movement of the producer into the spotlight, from Spector to Brian Wilson, James Brown, and Motown; to disco auteurs Cerrone and Don Ray; to Kraftwerk and Afrika Bambaata; to Prince, Dr. Dre, Kanye West, and Daft Punk. And that's more than a nerdy pop footnote. It's not the only way, but it's one big way to think about how the technology and the art

Tom Smucker

tie together; and it helps explain, for instance, why DJ-producer and Roots bandleader Questlove is a Beach Boys, Brian Wilson, and *Pet Sounds* fan.[5] They're all in that same chronology.

Working from two different traditions, by the late '60s, James Brown and Brian Wilson found themselves in the same place: in control in the studio; able to produce singles ready for radio play or to stretch out on LPS, far beyond songs arranged from sheet music; thinking about a recording as a presentation of sonic textures; and ready to create "Cold Sweat" and "Good Vibrations." At their peak, both could imagine how they wanted their music to sound as a recording coming out of a car radio or home stereo. And both understood the technicalities of the recording studios at the time, as well as the personalities and abilities of the other musicians. They understood their own strengths and limitations, and the expectations of their audiences. It was as if the director, screenwriter, and star of the movie were all the same person.

Which brings us back to the kid at the band shell with the laptop. When added to the lineup onstage, that kid doesn't replace all the previous acts. Next up might even be a folk singer with an acoustic guitar, who put together a repertoire by downloading old recordings from Appalachia onto a laptop. Changes in technology can play out in more than one direction over time, depending on human beings and their cultural requirements, economic options, and desires.

....

The technical, artistic, and social coming-of-age of the studio-produced LP, including *Pet Sounds*, was indeed something big, new, and wonderful that got all tangled up in the '60s in lots of good ways, with the social and political upheavals of the times and the arrival of us baby boomers at adolescence and young adulthood. New art for a new generation. But when the energy uncapped by this combination got mistaken for an inevitable new dawn of ever-increasing spiritual enlightenment and artistic and social progress, the Beach Boys found themselves devalued by two different put-downs. Members of the Beatles-enraptured wing of the white rock counterculture tastemaker establishment accused the Boys of foolishly daring to challenge the rock royalty from Liverpool (and failing).[6] Sensitive white-guy rock theorists and devotees of Brian Wilson descended into a public and personal funk when their patience was not rewarded, and their need for ever more transcendent LPs wasn't sated, and *Smile* was not released.[7] The Beach Boys had dared to go too far and not dared to go far enough. Believing either of these conclusions led to missing out on a lot of great music.

After shelving *Smile*, the Boys moved into recording as a group in Brian's home studio. So ends stage one of Brian as composer-producer-arranger lead singer rock Mozart (stage two would commence in 1988 with his solo career). And so begins the more or less produced-by-the-group era, beginning with a three-album cycle of homespun explorations of the studio's potential.

Smiley Smile captures this moment. The hit singles at the top of the two vinyl sides, "Heroes and Villains" and "Good Vibrations," are the last of the big, multilayered studio recordings. The rest of the cuts dismantle those hits into fragments and what we imagine could also be bits from *Smile*—like hearing the bebop version of a standard when no one's ever heard the standard;

Tom Smucker

or discovering indie rock before there's any indie rock; or some very hip but ridiculous, technically manipulated a capella vocal jazz, what any group of stoners might sound like today if they were hanging out with Pro-Tools and one of them was a genius and all of them were the greatest white harmony singers on the planet. As if to say, "*This* is our next step in the studio after *Pet Sounds* and it isn't *Smile*."

Three months after *Smiley Smile* came *Wild Honey*, back to basics and peculiar enough to stay interesting, muddy, almost low-fi white r&b. Six months after that came *Friends*, a mellow, domestic return to *Pet Sounds*–style production. In less than a year after *Smile* was abandoned, the Beach Boys threw off three unique and wonderful albums that still sound like the Beach Boys, creativity that fell through the cracks if you were stuck thinking about rock music always *advancing*. These were the best nine months ever for an unsteady fan (me) to be moved to a public lifetime commitment, or some might say obsession.

All three albums hold up today as proof of the band's versatility and charm. And when released, all three failed to connect with the larger public the Beach Boys saw slip away. Some of that was the Age of Aquarius gone-sour disappointment of the *Smile* devotees. Some of that was the readjustment inside the group to Brian's slow abdication from recording and from life. Some of that was the music's modest presentation. Some of it was an old Beach Boys problem—inattention to album art and other visual signaling. What was the *Wild Honey* cover telling you, if anything, about the contents? And some of it was the timing. I couldn't listen to *Friends* much when it first came out in 1968 because it was, you know, 1968, the least mellow year ever in North America, Vietnam, Mexico, and Europe. Freed by the passage of time from being linked to that moment, *Friends* works when you want it to now.

The 1967–1968 period was a great time for a hard-core fan. Every new album was different, yet interesting. The concerts were always wonderful, and it was easy to get tickets. I would have been happy if the Beach Boys had kept this version of themselves forever, and they did for two more albums, *20/20* and *Sunflower*.

But they had been a big band from a big time and place, early '60s Southern California, and they now stood for a time and place—the past. By the '70s, the Boys were looking for a comeback; they needed to make a big statement that proved they were at least near the center of the action, and the times demanded hip relevance. The Kingston Trio shirts were dumped, and the Boys grew long hair and beards. Jack Rieley came on board as manager and helped write profound or at least of-the-era lyrics for their up-to-date new albums. They switched record labels, paid close attention to the album covers, shared the stage at the Fillmore East with the Grateful Dead, played at the huge antiwar 1971 May Day rally in Washington, DC, and cultivated a connection with contemporary surf culture.

Surf's Up in 1971, *Holland* in 1973, and *The Beach Boys in Concert* in 1973 brought them back into or at least near the limelight. You didn't even need to listen to the *In Concert* album, because the double record cover told the story: this was one up-to-date-looking rock band, with two new members from South Africa, not an oldies act. And the playlist proved it: the Boys had integrated their group and their old and new songs—an accomplishment of their ongoing studio output, and maybe more important, of their ability to pull it all together onstage.

Mike Love was always the front man, willing to work the crowd and add between-song commentary, the antidote to the rest of the band's natural reserve or plain lack of stage presence. If you weren't getting the message that the group had updated by noting the other band members' Byrds- and Dead-style duds, then Mike's flowing robes, his rockin' guru concert wardrobe, convinced you that the striped Kingston Trio shirts were never returning.

As the bandleader by default after Brian bowed out, Carl had to work a bigger ensemble into the live act as the studio recordings moved away from guitar-based rock, while his own guitar playing held the transitions together from Chuck Berry to jazz to orchestral-style changes, alongside his versatile, beautiful, expressive-when-appropriate vocals, both solo and in harmony, as always the strongest link between the Beach Boys' old and new music, the connective tissue that held together the splits of the Sixties.

When they first hit and were stretching out their sets with other surf standards, along with "Johnny B. Goode" and "What'd I Say," the group's ability to duplicate their vocals in person distinguished them from a cover band. When Brian's compositions evolved and Carl had to figure out how to transpose that onto the stage, their vocals ensured continuity. When Brian quit touring, it helped that all their voices were close in pitch and timbre, and Carl sounded just like Brian, only better. And when they had to incorporate the early hits, the quirky tracks, the near hits, and the early '70s profound and arty showpieces into their early '70s concerts, it mattered that vocally, they still sounded like themselves across all this material, that they could still sing "Their Hearts Were Full of Spring" in person, a capella, without Brian.

Catching them in concert in the early '70s when they were on their way back up and had something to prove, you heard a tight, confident live band that presented an enormous variety of music from across their entire career. For a while, they were so confident that they would start the evening with "Good Vibrations," making a statement: we've got enough good stuff to use our finale for the opener.

The Temptations made their own early to late '60s transition, from Smokey Robinson to Norman Whitfield songs and production, from "My Girl" to "Ball of Confusion" and "Cloud Nine." This was both a switch from classic Motown pop to Sly Stone and Isaac Hayes–influenced psychedelic funk and a move from New Frontier, civil rights movement era optimism to ghetto realism, a divide that survives in their live shows today, alongside their third stream, the Copacabana/Supper Club "Hello Young Lovers" repertoire.

And here's where the Beach Boys (and the Temptations) moved through history differently than their counterparts from New Jersey. The Four Seasons weren't idealists or big-picture guys; they were realists, born into hierarchies, not endless horizons. I'm a poor boy, not good enough for you, so leave me, they could shout. Their albums might have a theme—Folk, Broadway, a Dylan tribute—but did not announce a concept or phase or stake a claim to some history. Working solo or with the Seasons, Frankie Valli would continue to release hits through the

'70s, but missed fitting into any of the categories that would give shape to the group's story until *Jersey Boys* landed on Broadway in 2006.

By 1974, the year they released *Endless Summer*, the Beach Boys were back to being certifiably with-it, *Rolling Stone*'s Band of the Year, without producing any new material. Their career stretched from pre-Beatles to post-Beatles pop, and they had learned how to present it all live in concerts, with audiences eating it up. If all the pieces didn't quite fit together—and sometimes there were loose ends—this only proved that they were still the Average Joes they had been when they first started out, doing their best to stay afloat through all the changes: less like all-knowing, all-powerful rock gods, and more like neighborhood hippies, at times full of nonsense, just like their audience, us.

....

Although the group efforts on *Surf's Up* and *Holland* were critical and popular successes and set the stage for the public's recognition of the Boys' earlier work on *Endless Summer*, it was that anthology of the old stuff, from when Brian was doing the writing and producing, that went number one and stayed there, and that changed the band. The created-by-Brian and influenced-by-Brian but in some ways post-Brian collaborative band that had produced so much good music from *Smiley Smile* through *Holland* was eclipsed and retired, replaced by the Brian-Is-Back or the Bring-Brian-Back-and-Have-Him-Write-Another-Endless-Summer-Big-Hit band.

For the *Holland* album, Brian had been essentially banished to a bonus seven-inch disc where he mourned the loss of his muse on "Mount Vernon and Fairway."[8] The disc was taped to the outside cover, while the rest of the band was busy inside the LP solidifying their newly acquired hip status. Then the *Endless Summer* sales tsunami landed. By 1976, Brian had been placed (or forced) into the saddle in the studio by his shrink, the record company, and some of his bandmates, in the hope of producing some new *Endless Summer*–style hits. The result, *The Beach Boys Love You*, was released in 1977. A Brian-produced, Brian-recorded, Brian-on-synths in-the-studio album, tweaked and cleaned up by Carl, with at least one perfect vocal from Mike ("Johnny Carson"), *Love You* contains some grim to weird sentiments hiding under a cracking façade of bare-bones synth rock and lighthearted pop. Brian was finally alone and in charge in the studio (with the ominous retinue of his domineering therapist lurking in the shadows), but we didn't get *Smile Part Two* or *Pet Sounds Part Two* or *Endless Summer Part Two*. Sometimes it's touching, sometimes it's funny, sometimes it's upsetting, sometimes it's rough, but the music never sounds boring. And as it turned out, this post-utopian studio combo matched late '70s punk, early new wave, and soon-to-arrive indie rock enough to score kudos from Peter Buck of REM and Patti Smith.[9]

Too peculiar to produce any chart-topping singles or have much of an impact on concerts, *Love You* generated valuable late '70s artistic credibility, positioned the Beach Boys' more off-beat post–*Pet Sounds* albums for positive reevaluations, and set a starting point for Brian's future solo career. *Love You* would also be the last interesting full-length new studio album the Beach Boys would ever release. Their final six albums, if you don't count compilations and old concerts from the vault, have their moments, including the great one with "Kokomo," but more often than not, they run out of steam before the end of a song, and sometimes there is no steam at all.

In 1994, Brian would meet his talented power pop acolytes, the Wondermints, backstage at a concert and recruit them as the core of his new band, which performed *Pet Sounds* live on tour beginning in 2000. The former studio recluse became a concert draw by not being dead, and was now accepted as a tortured genius who had somehow survived. Then, in 2004, with help from this band and some old and new collaborators, came the biggest surprise of his career: thirty-seven years after he shelved it, Brian Wilson completed *Smile*, took it on tour, and recorded and released the CD. The tale of this completion is told elsewhere, but what's noteworthy here is that *Smile* was first performed in full in concert and then recorded and released, reversing the old pop order of studio creation first, followed by live presentation. Maybe *Smile* was premiered this way for maximum impact, or maybe the money was now made from the tour and not from the recording. Or maybe guitar and keyboard technology had advanced far enough to make layered studio recording unnecessary. Or maybe the studio had turned into a maze, with too many options and opportunities and demands that first had to be escaped and avoided to finally bring Brian's masterpiece to the public. Whatever the reason, for the first time in decades, Brian was active onstage and in the studio.

5

Fathers, Shrinks, and Gurus

....

When Murry Wilson, father of the Wilson brothers and uncle of Mike Love, died at age fifty-five, the Beach Boys released a eulogy that included these sentences: "Murry Wilson was a hard oyster shell of a man, aggressively masking a pushover softness which revealed itself at the sound of a beautiful chord or the thought of his wife and three sons . . . In his eyes they remained 'boys' until the end, though Brian is now 30, Dennis 28, and Carl 26. They were not the 'tough' men he used to say he wanted them to be but, over his last years, Murry Wilson whittled down the generation gap through increased confidence in all three, despite their 'soft' ways."[1]

Ten years into the band's career, the tyrannical sadist, sentimental old softie, and ambitious parent who had launched his children into rock-and-roll fame was described in the Beach Boys' own press release as a hard man appeased by music from his soft boys. Yet they had to fire that hard dad as a manager and studio meddler before the music by their soft older brother could fully flower. And then that competent, inspired, dominant but soft older brother withdrew. From everything.

On one level, this Beach Boys story fascinates because of the father-son struggle and the eldest son's abdication—conflicts as old as the Bible. On another level lies the thrill of the cheap exposé. Although the "sunny good times" label never felt accurate, it has stuck to the Boys throughout their five decades plus, often with their connivance, making periodic exposés inevitable.

White Southern California teenagers in the early 1960s weren't supposed to need to rebel; they met the expectations of the affluence their parents had worked and fought for by creating their own leisure space and culture, and the Beach Boys sang from inside these assumptions. And here's where it gets past the biblical to something more twentieth-century American. First, Brian Wilson succeeded at something his father helped make possible. And then he fired his own father, who couldn't really follow where his sons had gone. Affluence and upward mobility allowed the children to meet their father's expectations and become the people their father resented, as they transitioned from suburban strivers to rich Hollywood artists. Played out in the world of white rock and roll, it's what sociologist Richard Sennett labeled the hidden injuries of class.[2] The child unintentionally but inevitably humiliates the parent by meeting the parent's expectations for the child's upward mobility, leaving the parent behind.

This paradox also includes a musical layer. Murry was often an unhinged version of a Frank Sinatra–style tough guy protecting a sensitive interior. Biographies and interviews describe an irrational patriarch who the sons could sometimes soothe with their beautiful music. But his own album on Capitol in 1967, *The Many Moods of Murry Wilson*, isn't sensitive tough-guy stuff at all. It's a rather sentimental, slightly melancholy tour of easy-listening instrumentals, which Murry describes on the back cover as "mixed as emotionally as possible." By extending the definition of "as possible," the sons overthrew the father by fully realizing his own music. Check out the instrumentals on *Pet Sounds*.

The father who was fired dies young, in 1973, when Brian is well into his own withdrawal. It had been overwhelming to become the dominant soft son, and now the hard dad was gone. And here their story meshes with a larger Sixties story that's been with us ever since, another portion of Beach Boys history that sticks inside our shared history.

Fathers and father figures are in trouble. A rapidly changing culture and economy, the result of a world the fathers achieved, is creating a new world in which fatherly wisdom and experience don't apply. At the same time, the civil rights movement, the Vietnam War, the changes in sexual norms call into question the authority of existing father figures. Have all the presidents been lying to us all along about the light at the end of the tunnel of the Vietnam War?

No one's in charge, and everyone can do their own thing. A lot of positive space opens up, but so does some negative space. At the most modest level, I recall being one of a group of stoned hippies sitting around on a living room floor, listening to a record. And then the record ends, and someone has to get up and turn the record over or pick a different album. That person can go on to become a DJ (good) or that manipulative, take-charge, countercultural creep you drift away from if you're sensible and lucky. But someone has to take charge and get up and pick out the next record.

In a group with no mechanism for making decisions, you get charisma instead of chain of command; you get the domineering, groovy boyfriend; you get Dennis Wilson's nearly fatal friendship with the mass-murdering mastermind in hippie clothing, Charles Manson; you get Brian Wilson's decades with the unethical, greedy, destructive therapist Dr. Eugene Landy; you get the group's mixed-bag relationship with the celebrity guru Maharishi Mahesh Yogi. And you get the ongoing flailing of the Sixties by conservatives.

I don't begrudge the Beach Boys or anyone else their sorting through Sixties culture to make sense of their changing circumstances, and I don't want to sweep under the rock-and-roll rug some of the really bad choices that were made by them and for them. But I dislike the critique that blames those really bad choices on making any choices at all, and that doesn't care to look at the circumstances in which those choices were made or why those circumstances changed. As that put-down would have it, the Beach Boys booted their dad as manager and producer because they were affluent and spoiled and raised without discipline and didn't want anyone in charge of anything. But in reality, they booted him out because the eldest brother was a genius, and they had engaged with a new technology and culture and understood it better than their dad. They were "soft" not in spite of, but because of their father. They soothed him with songs, they elevated his music, they worked to fulfill his ambitions. But how could they replace him when they had to? How could they replace Brian when he checked out? These issues aren't wrestled with by just a small subset of their fans. These are wrestled with in our bigger culture, all the way up to our choice of president. What do you do when the father figures disappear or get discredited?

Beach Boys music rarely addressed these themes directly. It wasn't designed for conflict or confrontation. Brian's "I'm Bugged at My Ol' Man" from *Summer Days (And Summer Nights!!)* was sung and written with ironic quotes around it, in atypical, informal Elvis-imitator mode, with enough exaggeration to mask its close relation to reality. When group folkie Al Jardine got to sing "The Times They Are A-Changin'" straight on the *Beach Boys' Party!* sessions, it got released with fake-live, overdubbed crowd noise goofing on the words. When Dennis explored a more aggressive rocker persona, he got as far as clamoring for sex. Mike wrote a song about avoiding student demonstrations.

The conclusion to "Surf's Up" comes closest to a Beach Boys kind of resolution, a truth achieved through Van Dyke Parks's so-poetical-you-aren't-sure-you-understand-them lyrics. After mentioning tough men who can't cry and the sound of children, the song ends by quoting William Wordsworth's 1802 line about the child being the father to the man.

Wordsworth was reinforcing the Christian ideal of childlike piety for grown-up believers. In a more secular context, so were Wilson and Parks. But I hear another interpretation in "Surf's Up," bubbling out of the affluent American Sixties, where the child might be forced into being father to The Man: a goal, a reality, and a curse. In a rapidly changing culture and technology, the child becomes father to the father, a burden so great that sometimes the child withdraws. "Surf's Up" offers a way out, the bottom-line Beach Boys solution, a willful, achieved innocence that it might take a lifetime to achieve, that requires the wisdom to distinguish from willful ignorance.

The Beach Boys moved along, firing and rehiring managers,

feuding, dying, over-medicating, suing each other, and surviving in one form or another—recorded or alive or reissued or repackaged, always at odds about who was in charge—until Dennis and Carl were gone and Mike and Brian were left in their two separate bands. Never claiming a position in the vanguard of the sexual revolution, the Beach Boys' struggles to express and maintain a vulnerable masculinity placed their story inside many of the last half century's changes, another reason their music and their history maintain their potency. They are more than a big band that stumbled and had a comeback. They are the soft boys of the hard dad.

6

Girlfriends, Wives, and Mothers

....

Three mothers helped create the Beach Boys. Al Jardine's mother fronted the money so they could rent instruments and make their first recordings. Mike Love's mother, who was Murry Wilson's sister, threw Mike out of the house for getting his girlfriend pregnant, and this motivated the new family man to search for better work than pumping gas. The Wilson brothers' mom, Audree, a sometime shelter from their tempestuous dad Murry, was a bedrock source of much of the Beach Boys sound. She taught Brian boogie-woogie piano, a form that allowed the left-hand bass figure to modify the chords established by the right.[1]

The Beach Boys were a girl group, where the singer could also be the composer and producer and a guy. This opened up a space for the soft boys of the previous chapter to express their girl group anxieties and insecurities and desires for romantic validation. In the rock era, there were plenty of sad or dramatic songs about breaking up, more often by women than by men, but not many by white men about being *anxious* about breaking up, about the man worrying that the woman might leave or disappear.

At his peak, Brian combined a confidence in the studio with an ability to express an insecure masculinity redeemed by a woman's love in a two-and-a-half-minute pop rock song. The magic in the music made this expression a triumph, not a defeat. And that's really at the heart of "Help Me Rhonda," the rocker that's become an encore singalong for most Beach Boys–based concerts, including Brian Wilson's.

Female idealization is its own trap—what if the woman can't or doesn't want to resolve every problem that the guy presents? Or what if the guy is addicted to falling in love with an idealization, and then must move on to a new idealization whenever reality sets in? Those are, at least, a different set of issues than the ones raised by heterosexual pop misogyny: cock rock obsessions about regaining and maintaining domination, rock star masculinized bisexuality that absorbs and controls all sexual energy and leaves the woman (or underage girl) with no agency, or the reverse-twist declaration of macho vulnerability: "I am the most vulnerable man in existence, more vulnerable than any woman could ever hope to become." These are issues of power and control.

At their best, the Beach Boys songs about anxiety and romance explore negotiations between innocence, idealization, reality, need, and risk—not power. The greatest early-career, pre–*Pet Sounds* expression of this negotiation is a (sort of) car song, "Don't Worry Baby." The concrete details describe the protagonist's girlfriend reassuring him about an upcoming drag race. But the wordless harmony intro and Brian's emotional, high-stakes, falsetto vocal establish this womanly reassurance, not the outcome of the race, as being what's at stake in the song's desperate resolution. The competition details don't even come out until the second verse. The protagonist has set up a potential catastrophe with his male bragging that underlines his ongoing sense of dread, and he is the grateful receiver, not dispenser, of sexual love in the third verse. Even the instrumental break maintains a pop stateliness for this drama, with plucked string staccatos and repetitive chord changes. This is not the time for a sax, guitar, organ, or drum solo, often used to signify rock male exuberance.

There are other examples from the early and mid-'6os, and they are not limited to obscure cuts. Returning the early songs to mid-'70s prominence, both the mega-selling North American compilation *Endless Summer* and the UK version *20 Golden Greats* contain "Don't Worry Baby" and "Help Me Rhonda" as well as "You're So Good To Me." All three float in the mainstream of shared Beach Boys memories on both sides of the Atlantic.

These pleasures and dilemmas reached their fullest expression on *Pet Sounds*. By the time *Wild Honey* was released in 1967 —the wonderful white r&b, back-to-basics retrenchment after *Smile*'s nonappearance—the Beach Boys had moved past adolescent agony to a positive, affectionate young adult perspective on sex and romance. *20/20* in 1969 is a potluck of perspectives, with Dennis in Charles Manson mode and Brian in mellow withdrawal.

Sunflower, in 1970, presented band members as relaxed, affluent, pop-hippie fathers, possibly divorced, with their babies on the cover and a spectrum of responses to romance and sex in the grooves. For some of us, this was a nearly perfect album that failed to connect with the counterculture, failed commercially, and failed to induce the Beach Boys themselves to continue the pursuit of domestic stability in reality or in their music. One such possibility arose when Brian's first wife Marilyn and her sister Dianne released a beautiful pop album as *Spring* in 1972. Brian's involvement is most likely limited to four tracks, but it sounds like a Beach Boys record, and it contains covers of Beach Boys tracks like "Forever" and "This Whole World" from *Sunflower*. In some alternate universe, *Spring* could have begun a dialogue with *Sunflower* and integrated actual women into the group, but that's not how things worked out on planet Earth.

With *The Beach Boys Love You* in 1977, Brian's inner turmoil tugged at the heart but no longer matched up with his audience's romantic, sexual, and interpersonal realities. Soon the group would begin a sleepwalk through a decade performing the *Endless Summer* set list, as those old songs, if not the group itself, continued to speak to and for their fans.

And then, unpredictably, decades later, there was more.

Among the many surprises the new millennium brought from Brian, there was a new song on an old theme. The essentially honest 2015 movie biopic *Love and Mercy* includes his "One Kind of Love," commissioned for the ending credit roll, written for his second wife, Melinda. Both the movie and the song returned to themes of male anxiety and psychic collapse, and a woman's redemptive, unconditional love, a decades-later update of "Don't Worry Baby."

In these retellings, Brian, Dennis, and Carl's mother Audree Wilson rarely reappears. She doesn't have to.

7

When Did the Early Sixties End?

....

I was sitting in my room, spring of 1965, listening to one of Chicago's Top 40 stations when the Beach Boys came on. Physical chills ran up and down my body, and I had a revelation: that this music was, more than any other, mine. Or maybe really, that this music was me. I've had decades of cultural, religious, erotic, interpersonal, and political flashes of personal insight since then, but never one so strong or so unexpected.

What was the song? "Do You Wanna Dance"? "Help Me Rhonda"? "Please Let Me Wonder"? I don't know. I don't think I even heard an entire song. It was just a phrase, a line, or maybe a wordless stretch of vocal harmony, and that instantaneous comprehension. You don't admit it, you may not like it, but you already do and will henceforth identify yourself with the music of the Beach Boys. And then I was out the door, maybe on my way somewhere. Or maybe I just didn't want any more revelations.

The following winter, trying to understand this identity insight, I purchased the recently released *Beach Boys' Party!* in a Sears department store on the South Side of Chicago. It didn't grab me; it didn't even touch me. But the revelation had been a powerful experience, so the following year I tried again, and bought and listened to *Pet Sounds*. I was stunned and listened again. The final test: a listen on acid. And yes, that proved it. I had entered someplace deep.

In the United States, the Beach Boys' hugely successful mid-'70s compilation *Endless Summer* contained tracks from 1962 to 1965. In the UK, their similarly successful mid-'70s compilation, *20 Golden Greats*, contained tracks from 1962 to 1969. The difference in the span of years was most likely related to differing contractual rights in different countries, but those differences mirrored different histories. Those dates made a statement.

Across the ocean, Beach Boys music could be heard as a representation of a uniquely American musical portrait that spread across the '60s and beyond, proof that British fans were better able to see the '60s as one larger pop music picture. Over here, the *Endless Summer* break at 1965 matched a larger break. That summer Bob Dylan went electric at Newport; that winter the Beatles released *Rubber Soul*. But on a political level, the two countries diverged. In the UK, the conscription for young men into National Service had ended in 1960, while the Vietnam era draft was beginning to reach into the lives of young men across America in 1965.

In time, I would come to appreciate the *Party* album I'd purchased at that Sears, especially as an informal summing-up of influences past and present from the Everly Brothers to the Beatles. At the moment I bought it, that summing-up would not have been enough for me. When I got my Top 40 revelation, I knew only one person who smoked pot, and the war in Vietnam was a political issue not a personal reality. By the time I bought *Pet Sounds*, I only knew one person who did not smoke pot, and I was realistically contemplating going to Vietnam or jail. I had not changed cities, neighborhoods, or friends; the pot smoking was a symptom of the change, not a cause.

Chopped off sometime in 1965, the Beach Boys' career up to that moment can be fit into a variety of political and cultural interpretations, one reason that music can still draw crowds to concerts and streaming playlists. As for me, I find both the *Endless Summer* and *20 Golden Greats* track lists to be accurate summations. I know I experienced something called the early '60s, and it ended after *Beach Boys Party*. Then something different but not disconnected started, and *Pet Sounds* was near that beginning.

I completed my early Beach Boys collection in the late '60s cut-out bins of midtown Manhattan record stores as the Beach Boys were spinning off their quirky, engaging, sorry-no-*Smile*, post–*Pet Sounds* albums. So I was listening forward and backward from *Pet Sounds* at the same time. That record was the divide, but a divide that was also a connection, one that made me think the Beach Boys had a history, existed across a time. And when I listened for that history, I could hear it. If *Surfin' USA* and *Wild Honey* had sounded the same, with no *Pet Sounds* in between, then the Beach Boys could have had a collection of hits, but not a chronology. And trying to think through the Sixties required a culture that could provide a useful, believable chronology.

8

Jan and Dean

....

In 1959, the novelty doo-wop "Baby Talk" was the first hit single for West Los Angeles University "Uni" High School classmates Jan Berry and Dean Torrence. (Fellow alums: David Cassidy, Sandra Dee, John Densmore, Kim Fowley, Kim Gordon, Bruce Johnston, Jack Jones, Gidget, Randy Newman.) At least two histories repeat a hard-to-believe anecdote: on their first big summer tour in 1960, Jan and Dean were booked with Little Willie John, Bobby Day, and the Little Richard Band because the promoters and the audience thought that any group that sang doo-wop like that had to be black.[1] Playing it up, they would take the stage in the dark, and the spotlight would come on only after they'd started singing.

After 1963's "Linda," the duo ran out of concepts, but Lou Adler and Liberty records knew they had a potent, marketable persona. Tall, athletic blondes (Jan bleached his hair to match Dean's), casually dressed, ready to sell California's outdoorsy, affluent, white Protestant doo-wop and whatever came next. A high-IQ rich kid, Jan owned shelves of alphabetized 45s and two Ampex tape recorders when Dean first teamed up with him, so Jan already had the ability to overdub them into full four-part harmony. After sharing a bill with the then two-hit Beach Boys

73

at a concert, and borrowing them as a backing band, Jan and Dean got from Brian a half-finished song with the new concept the duo was looking for—singing about surfing—and Dean polished up the surfer lingo needed to complete the lyrics. Jan shared his studio smarts with Brian, and suggested that he start using professional studio musicians like the Wrecking Crew. Brian's and Jan and Dean's collaboration "Surf City" went number one in the summer of 1963, with Brian and Dean double tracked on the falsetto leads. This was followed by the Beach Boys' own hit "Surfin' USA."

Murry Wilson was pissed that Brian had shared his songwriting genius with someone outside the family, but the confident male heterosexual optimism of "Surf City" would have been a bad fit with the Beach Boys' developing mixture of romantic idealization, anxiety, loneliness, and relief.

Every bit as clever and sophisticated as Brian in their studio productions, Jan and Dean would remain the jokesters of vocal surf and hot rod rock, happy to find their hits and move along with the trends. *Jan & Dean Take Linda Surfin'*, *Drag City*, *Jan and Dean Meet Batman*, *Filet of Soul*, *Folk 'n Roll*. But the sincerity of later '60s folk rock and the oppositional politics and music in the air rubbed the patriotic fun seeker Jan the wrong way. Too much the wrong way for Dean, who removed his own name from the 1965 "Universal Coward" single, Jan's cold-warrior reply to Donovan's hit cover of Buffy Saint-Marie's pacifist "Universal Soldier." Jan and Dean's 1965 slightly schizo *Folk 'n Roll* LP included that track, along with "Eve of Destruction," "Turn, Turn, Turn," and "It Ain't Me Babe." But they did manage one old-style Jan and Dean joke on that album: "Folk City," an update of their "Drag City" update of their "Surf City" hit. From shooting the curl to a Blue Coral wax job to a Hohner harmonica.

Post-Korea, pre-Vietnam, Dean had completed his obligations with his draft board at Fort Ord while Jan had been busy with his career. Safe with a deferment as a premed college student at UCLA, Jan visited his draft board after receiving an induction notice and apparently was told that the armed forces needed doctors, so he would be drafted that year after graduation. The details are hard to pin down because after leaving the draft board on April 12, 1966, Jan totaled his Stingray, almost died, and never really recovered.[2] Jan and Dean would begin touring again in the late '70s as an oldies act, sometimes with the Beach Boys. Dean moved on to a career as a graphic designer, creating album covers and logos for the Beach Boys and many others, and after Jan's passing in 2004, Dean continued his performing and designing activities, sometimes teaming up with Mike Love. But the crash ended the plans for Jan and Dean's new record label, a TV show to rival the Monkees, a possible movie, any new records—and any chance to see how Jan and Dean would have maneuvered through the late '60s and into the '70s.

The coincidences are so obvious they're eerie. Jan and Dean had a huge hit with 1964's "Dead Man's Curve," a car-crash song with sound effects and a morbid narration, that Dean describes as Jan's masterpiece.[3] And then the "Universal Coward" single and the visit to the draft board . . .

Before it all ended, Dean would repay the debt to the Beach Boys for the gift of "Surf City." Depending on who's telling the story, on September 23, 1965, Dean was either taking a break, or bored or disgusted with the track Jan was working on down the hall at Western Recording in Hollywood, and he dropped into another studio, where the Beach Boys were finishing up their *Beach Boys' Party!* sessions. Dean either joined in on or suggested "Barbara Ann," the Regents' 1961 hit that Jan and Dean covered on *Jan & Dean's Golden Hits*, which, for the record, were essentially golden hits by other acts. Loosening things up just a bit, adding some swing, some syncopation, rich Beach Boys harmonies, and vocal dexterity, it was finished in three takes and edited down later for single radio play. Dean's double falsetto lead with Brian, originally deployed on "Surf City," propelled "Barbara Ann" to become the second-best-selling Beach Boys single ever; it was a simplified but glorious dramatization of the individual and the group, suitable for sing-alongs, convincing proof of devotees' claims that doo-wop was the real postwar urban folk music. And that's how a quickie recording from 1958 in the Bronx, which sat on the shelf for three years before its first go-round as a hit, became the continuous concert closer for two or three, sometimes four (Brian's, Mike's, Al's, and Dean's) different versions of two interrelated groups from Southern California.

9

Innocence and the Second-Best Pop Album Ever

....

On the evening of November 18, 2000, I left my wife and friends midway through a blues concert on Manhattan's Upper West Side and took the subway down to a Times Square club to catch the first tour of Brian Wilson and his band performing the entire *Pet Sounds* album live. I didn't go because I thought the show that night would be too good to miss. And I didn't go because I thought it would be a notable and interesting failure worth reviewing. I went because I am a fan, and barring births, deaths, and weddings, I attend every show related to the Beach Boys that comes my way.

But here's the twist. The blues concert had been a stifling affair, the white liberal audience as silent and respectful of the black musicians as a Mozart audience at Carnegie Hall. Fifty blocks downtown, Brian Wilson and his band's successful recreation of a thirty-five-year-old vinyl LP had that audience in a happy uproar, shouting out with pleasure every time an impossible melodic tidbit was played live from the stage.

How did this happen? Where did an audience come from that sounded like the one on B.B. King's *Live at the Regal* for a white pop so far removed from the blues?

It wasn't easy to figure out what was going on with *Pet Sounds* if you were browsing at a record store back when the album was first released in 1966. The front cover showed the Boys in contemporary Beatles era haircuts and clothes, feeding goats at a zoo. The back featured some black-and-white concert shots with the group once again in their outdated Kingston Trio striped shirts, Brian sitting alone at a piano, and some unexplained pictures either taken in Japan or, quite possibly, I worried at the time, mocking Japanese culture somewhere in North America. If you've seen the *Love and Mercy* movie, you know the real story: the rest of the group was touring Japan while Brian composed and produced the instrumental tracks for *Pet Sounds* in the studio. And you know the title referred to all the sounds deployed on the record—vocal, instrumental, and otherwise, including Brian's dogs barking at a train after the last song, "Caroline No."

That connection might have been easier to grasp if the group had posed in the studio with Brian's dogs. Goats at zoos aren't even pets. The only reference to Japan on any of their previous records was "Little Honda," and none of this was explained or clarified in a back-cover blurb, as was common in those days on jazz, classical, and folk albums. Bob Dylan marked his own journey from folk poet to beatnik rock god with self-penned back-cover essays. Beach Boys consumers were on their own.

Fifty years later, it's possible to consider the *Pet Sounds* cover photos so oddball they're hip, but at the time, the goat feeding looked like an off-kilter teen magazine dream-date photo shoot, especially when compared to Dylan or the groovy, distorted Beatles on the front cover of *Rubber Soul*. In fact, *Pet Sounds*' lyrics really were at times adolescent. But if this was a teen dream, when you really listened, it was one with more peculiar, unsettling depth than that cover could convey.

Early Beach Boys album art made it clear when they were singing about surfing, cars, or summer. The covers were less successful at signifying the Boys' turn toward songs about relationships and inner turmoil. *The Beach Boys Today!*, a 1965 preview of the themes and style of *Pet Sounds*, displayed a smiling lineup of the Boys in matching sweaters, more a cover-up than a clue. By then, the Beatles, the Stones, Dylan, and the Temptations were pondering and scowling on their record covers.

In time, rock fans would get past the cover photos and gain some idea about what was actually going on with the music, and would accept as a given the idea that *Rubber Soul* inspired Brian to create *Pet Sounds*, which inspired John and Paul to create *Sgt. Pepper*, a point reiterated by Beatles producer George Martin from the stage of Radio City Music Hall at the 2001 Brian Wilson Tribute. In the '60s, those dots weren't so easily connected for the record-buying public, myself included, and the two bands' mutual record label didn't help. With a corporate schizophrenia never really explained, Capitol Records was able to market the Beatles in the United States as hip, fun, serious, and arty. Slicing and dicing their UK albums before *Sgt. Pepper*, Capitol created albums easier to market in the States, re-jiggered for greater cultural impact. *Rubber Soul* had a more consistently folk rock track list in the States than in the UK and was released here without singles, a sign that this was not a mishmash of pop hits and filler. This was Art, like classical or jazz. But Capitol undercut the suspiciously arty and self-contained *Pet Sounds* by releasing *Best of the Beach Boys Volume 1* only two months later in the States. Offering eleven great older singles and one ringer (their version of "Louie, Louie"), *Best of the Beach Boys* knocked *Pet Sounds* down and then off the charts, to face at least a decade with a reputation as a failure. While over in the UK, the new album got a proper debut. Beach Boy Bruce Johnston, along with the publicist Derek Taylor, hustling LA pop music insider Kim Fowley, and the Who's Keith Moon were able to play a prerelease *Pet Sounds* for the impressed Lennon and McCartney and a hotel full of hangers-on, and create a buzz in London still activated more than five decades later.[1]

....

In 1966 the American rock consumer (me) faced another hurdle if we got past the goats at the zoo—on first listen, the music could sound both dense and shallow. Within the full, affluent texture that suffused the entire LP, each cut had its own individual, complex instrumentation. On top sat the vocals, with lyrics both mature and, well, sometimes immature and frequently gloomy. Like the cover photo, the music could be dismissed as odd and not immediately engaging. If you didn't really listen, it could be brushed off as just the Beach Boys with strings. But the music could also pull you in, compel a closer listen, and then hook you.

The happiest song opens the album: "Wouldn't It Be Nice," an update on their earlier cover of the Students' "So Young" or their own "We'll Run Away." An anticipation of married bliss, "Wouldn't It Be Nice" situates that domesticity still out of reach, like those "Girls On The Beach" from 1964's *All Summer Long.* So there's just a suggestion that the couple in the song is dreaming about something that may never happen.

The second happiest song is "Sloop John B," a revamp of the Kingston Trio's revamp of the Weavers' revamp of a Caribbean folk song about a shipwreck. Some purists bitch that "John B" was forced onto the album by Capitol, which was looking for a hit single. But if it's not a new Brian Wilson composition, "John B" has the same production feel and vocal mix as the rest of the album, and it echoes, with an up-tempo folkie vibe, the album's themes of bad trips, isolation, and exile, directly stating one of *Pet Sounds*' central laments: "I want to go home."

Over the decades, "God Only Knows," which opens side two of the original vinyl release, has made the slow crawl from B side of the "Wouldn't It Be Nice" single, to become a standard, if not the greatest song of the entire rock era. That status has been achieved in large part because it's really good, because Paul McCartney says so, because it has the stately demeanor befitting a standard, because Carl Wilson duplicated his stunning studio vocal lead thousands of times in concert, and because Brian stayed alive and returned to touring and presenting *Pet Sounds* in concert. In 2014, BBC Music produced an extravagant video of the song featuring Brian, Pharrell Williams, Elton John, Lorde, Stevie Wonder, Chrissie Hynde, Baaba Maal, David Grohl, and twenty other celebs. John Legend and Cynthia Erivo sang it on the in-memoriam segment of the 2017 Grammys. It's the grown-up resolution of "Don't Worry Baby."

Yet for me, the album's heart is "Don't Talk (Put Your Head on My Shoulder)," the celebration of an intimate, wordless moment when anticipations, anxieties, and sorrows disappear. The paradox of words expressing the inexpressible floats atop the most beautiful backing track of them all, a countermelody, cello and violin heaven punctuated with kettledrums and warmed with electric organ.

The next cut is one of two instrumentals, "Let's Go Away for Awhile," a soundtrack for a very short movie, drawing our attention to everything that's going on below the vocals, beyond the words, with progressions so tricky that Brian once bragged no one could hum them. Moving through changes in key, genre, instrumentation, and shtick, the track maintains a consistent deceptive mellow in shallow waters, hiding something lurking just below the surface. It's Beethoven Goes Hawaiian—Brian's brilliant, richer, disruptive realization of the easy-listening instrumentals that would appear on his father's 1967 *The Many Moods of Murry Wilson*. Easily skipped over by ears trained to ignore the assault of so-called elevator music, "Let's Go Away for Awhile" holds the key to *Pet Sounds*' genius as well as the album's erratic reputation in the United States.

It was one thing to appropriate Chicago Blues, Muddy Waters, and Howlin' Wolf, and to become the Rolling Stones. And it was one thing to appropriate string quartets on "Eleanor Rigby" and to be the Beatles. In a rock context, both of those were displays of good taste and artistic ambition. But it was something else to appropriate Percy Faith, Martin Denny, lounge, Tiki, faux jazz, cowboy songs, your dad's sentimentality; mix all that with Aaron Copland, George Gershwin, Phil Spector, Stephen Foster, and the Brill Building; and use a theremin, violins, kettledrums, electric organ, French horns, electric bass, string bass, a bicycle horn, rock guitars, keyboards, whistles, drum kits, bass harmonica, bongos, and vibes. And to place heartfelt, secular-spiritual, doo-wop-originated, jazz-inflected vocals on the top. That's what Brian Wilson achieved on *Pet Sounds*. He summoned up an enormous chunk of lower-middle-class, white, suburban '60s America, and made it swing.

Across the Atlantic Ocean, this mid-American cultural stew seemed to only signal sunny California pop ambition, but in the States among some of the public, including portions of the pop rock tastemaking gatekeepers, the manipulation of cornball schlock alongside rock authenticity and highbrow ambition sounded horrifying. Rockers were annoyed that the music didn't rock. Trad pop purists didn't like the way it strayed beyond the bounds of standards. I found it thrilling.

....

Pet Sounds is my favorite album, speaking to me, consoling me, and explaining me to myself for more than fifty years. It's an achievement for a culture from a certain time and place bound up with my own identity. More broadly, with time, and with the realization that the Brits weren't having any problems with the cultural residue, it was understood as a notable moment in the history of recorded music that explored and exploited the full potential of the studio. It's an example of one way to create rock-era pop that worked on many levels, that could absorb sounds and musical influences from everywhere and anywhere and remain coherent and accessible, with individual tracks that could work as pop singles while sounding like a part of an entire album.

But I've always been creeped out by fellow devotees who claimed a special sensitivity as fans and therefore claimed a special status for *Pet Sounds*. I believe the album gave Lennon and McCartney some big ideas. I believe it's possible to compare it in spirit and execution to Funkadelic's *One Nation under a Groove*.[2] But I never believed it should be everybody's favorite album. Or everybody's second-favorite album. Or that there was something insensitive about not responding to it at all. And I sometimes wonder if the album's long-term elevated reputation is really the result of a lot of sensitive old white men like me rising to positions of influence and power.

Much of the music the Beach Boys created before and after *Pet Sounds* was just as good and sometimes better. Check out *All Summer Long*, *Beach Boys' Party!*, *Smiley Smile*, and *Wild Honey*. That fact doesn't diminish the album but makes it special, placing it inside an accurate, impressive, and interesting context. Those five albums are all very different, all very Beach Boys, all holding their own after five decades.

When Brian was first toying with "Good Vibrations," many close to the group wanted it included on *Pet Sounds*, hoping to make the album a hit by piggybacking on that surefire single. But Brian refused. "Good Vibrations" is an optimistic Summer of Love masterpiece extending the boundaries of the pop music single, but it is not a personal statement. The singer of that song is an abstraction. *Pet Sounds* is album length and strength introspection, emotional vulnerability writ large; it revisits recurrent Beach Boys themes, especially the transition from falling into an ecstasy of idealization when falling in love, and then losing that idealization to the passage of time.

That gain and loss is all over the recording. It's in the anticipation that opens the album with "Wouldn't It Be Nice," and the sorrow in the album-closing "Caroline No." Placed alongside songs about psychological instability and physical dislocation, this sense of loss can't be dismissed as childish or charming. On such a deeply layered album, the losses feel linked—all a part of a larger loss, the loss of one kind of innocence.

Lots of us baby boomers grew up inside a post–Great Depression, post–World War II insistence on innocence that could easily become an insistence on denial—an imperative that Beach Boys music struggles to achieve and overcome. The affluence that spread across large swaths of the United States after the war was real, and so were the leisure pursuits that affluence created, and which were celebrated by the Beach Boys. Just as real were the traumas and the worries and the anxieties expressed in their songs: problems the affluence was supposed to cover up. *Pet Sounds* was a rebuke to that false affluent innocence on its own affluent turf, Brian's chance to fully articulate his anxieties as a part of his search for an honest innocence, using all of his pop music powers.

The early Beach Boys hadn't understood that their lower-middle-class suburban life wasn't important, so they sang as if it had been, and made it matter. By the time *Pet Sounds* was released, that kind of innocent discovery was locked away, still available inside those songs, but the Boys were too rich, too successful, too old, and the world had changed too quickly for them to access that Hawthorne reality to create something new. They had to move on, but where? Fame allowed new possibilities, and sealed off old options.

....

Murry, the Wilsons' savvy father, had hustled their contract at Capitol Records. Not at Vee-Jay, out of Chicago, where the Four Seasons first landed, where the Beatles' first stateside records were released, and which would then go kaput. Not at Liberty, which signed and then screwed around with Jan and Dean. Murry brought the Boys to secure, big-time Capitol. Then Brian (and probably Murry) realized that he could make better records at independent studios like Gold or Western, and Murry convinced Capitol to let Brian record where he wanted. But that was as far as the father's worldly wisdom and the son's genius could take them. Brian and the other Beach Boys did not know how to maneuver beyond that point, inside Capitol's vast corporate structure.

Brian had the budget and the free hand in the studio and the confidence and the desire, so while the rest of the group was off touring in Japan, he got to go deep inside himself while reaching far outside himself. Isolated in the studio, he was creating what he hoped would be another chart-topping album of pop music. To do so, he had to sustain an innocence about the outcome. He had to believe that the fans would come along, that Capitol would promote the album, and that his brothers and his cousin (and his father) would approve. While the music held onto those expectations, it also held onto a dread that the entire project could all fall apart, not only for Caroline and her long hair at album's end, but for the album itself. The train leaving the station might be passing all of us by: the listeners, the Beach Boys, Brian, his dogs.

In the short run, *Pet Sounds*' emotional honesty and musical ambition rested on a shaky trust in the powers that be to protect and promote the Beach Boys' new album that wasn't forthcoming. Capitol screwed Brian by releasing *Best of the Beach Boys*. In the much longer run, as it turned out, *Pet Sounds* survived and succeeded.

....

On first listen, the vocals on *Pet Sounds* can sound painful and pure and sometimes adolescent. Yet those vocals also hold the complex harmonies, chord changes, and melodies together on top of the fully realized instrumental tracks, and that is an expression of musical maturity.

Listened to on all these levels, *Pet Sounds* expresses a musicality that is confident about holding American culture together, from an individual worried that he may be falling apart. Readjust a bit, and you can hear an individual breaking under the strain of trying to hold his innocence about America together. That's what I heard in 1966 while thinking about my draft board choosing to send me overseas or to jail, and I wasn't the only one. I believe that's what, in their own way, the Capitol Records sales force heard as well; and I can imagine that, like so much else that was polarizing back then, this annoyed them or confounded them or scared them or pissed them off, so they wounded the record, almost fatally, with *Best of the Beach Boys*. It was marketing and promotion as sabotage, a forced return to an imagined and misunderstood optimistic American landscape. But the record recovered.

It recovered because it spun off two or three hits, because the Beach Boys stuck at it, and because they continued to release interesting music and perform interesting concerts until they returned to the spotlight, pulling *Pet Sounds* along. It recovered because it always had its defenders and advocates, moving inside and outside the structures of cultural power. And it recovered because the whole story of corporate neglect and artistic presentation matched up with mainstream ideas about the best art being at first misunderstood. And that matched up with struggles to come to terms with the Sixties, and with a country and culture at the peak of its power that stumbled and wasn't sure why or whether it wanted to know why.

....

Pet Sounds isn't the blues, but it shares one blues assumption. Acknowledging and singing about hard times and trouble won't make them disappear, but can help transcend them. For a couple of decades, one could worry that Brian Wilson himself had never recovered from making *Pet Sounds*, from experiencing its lukewarm US popularity and the corporate sabotage. Because he had not been touring back then, he missed out on experiencing the affection and enthusiasm the record generated and maintained in the UK. In light of his personal travails and the shaky reputation of *Pet Sounds*, it was easy to wonder if maybe the music had not led to transcendence for Brian, and hence, in pop artist and fan symbiosis, couldn't maintain the transcendence for us. Maybe we wouldn't recover.

In 1979, *The Rolling Stone Record Guide* counted *Pet Sounds* strong but spotty and rated it three stars out of five.[3] In 1983, *The New Rolling Stone Record Guide* counted *Pet Sounds* powerful but spotty and rated it four stars out of five.[4] In 2003, the December issue of *Rolling Stone* declared *Pet Sounds* the second-greatest rock album of all time.[5] All such canonizations are bogus, of course, when it comes down to culture that people find useful, but they do chart the changing evaluations of some of the rock-era gatekeepers and observers.

As *Pet Sounds* ascended out of semi-obscurity, Brian himself started touring. Seeing him and his new band play the whole album live proved that he had survived, and that his audience had survived; that a big chunk of '60s America could be embraced in its beauty, vulgarity, pain, and ignorance without defaulting to a false innocence or overwhelming despair; that the music could sometimes cut through the ignorance and transcend the pain; that the album was more than a moment when a musical genius exploited an extravagant budget; that it was a risk and an achievement, and it didn't need to be the second-best album ever to sustain that achievement. That's enough to make a room full of fans stand up and cheer, and not just in London.

10

Hip and White

....

There's all kinds of hip, but it's always about knowing at least two different, almost opposite realities at the same time. Elitists who don't know how the non-elites think aren't hip, they're just snobs. Inhabitants of the non-elite who only know their own world can be for real, but they're not hip. Cool kids who know how the non-cool kids think have a hip that might be as shallow as knowing what color socks the cool kids will be wearing to school the next day. That's close to the adolescent hip, where teenagers understand a separate reality as well as their parents' reality, a hip that disappears as they age.

Then there's a hip about a deeper knowledge, a reality that squares don't perceive. In a musical subculture like bebop or punk, there have to be the squares on the outside for there to be a hip inside. There have to be standards on which beboppers improvise their changes. There have to be rock excesses for punk rockers to be reacting against before there can be punk. There have to be parents who don't understand it for there to be rock and roll. And below it all lies the foundational, real American hip, the negotiation of what W. E. B. Du Bois named double-consciousness, the necessity of the oppressed to understand the way the oppressor sees them as well as how they see themselves.

Whether cool kids at school or globe-hopping rock stars, in their own way, the early Beach Boys were hip. Mike Love sang about it in "I Get Around." Most important, they came out of Southern California, and at that moment, SoCal was the mass culture's cutting edge. In their memoirs, both Mike Love of the Beach Boys and Dean Torrence of Jan and Dean recall being swept up at the beginning of their careers into the new national fascination with California. That made them hip. And they knew it.

We will never know how or whether Jan and Dean would have adjusted to mid-1960s changes, but the Beach Boys had to show they were aware of those changes if they were going to continue to exist inside pop culture. They had represented so much that now, they had to either figure out how to represent the present, or they would only represent the past. The Four Seasons weren't swimming in this symbolic pool. They continued to have hits. They were from New Jersey, but at the time the world wasn't interested in their New Jersey; the Seasons weren't interested in the rest of the world, and they didn't project themselves as conscious representations of New Jersey anyway.

The assassination of JFK, the end of the civil rights era, and the Vietnam War all raised questions about what was really true and what was false, about whether there was any shared consensus that everyone was working from, about whether presidents were lying and believed something different than what they were saying. How far you took all this depended on who you were, where you were from, and how you made sense of your life. But the times required pop music that reflected this disillusionment or confusion or combination of optimism and dread. Hip was a good generalization that could hold both what you thought had been true and what you believed true in the present.

A lot of less-than-brilliant music was produced. A lot of roads less taken turned out to be dead ends. Some pretensions wore out their welcomes earlier than others. The achievement of Woodstock was followed by the tragedy of Altamont. Charles Manson was Abbie Hoffman's doppelganger. Friends found themselves in the freedom of the Sixties, while others lost their way. But one reason the careers of the Beach Boys and Brian Wilson still hold our attention today is that they struggled along with their audience with the imperatives of hip as it was understood in white pop music of the '60s and '70s. Living through some of the hippie portion of the '60s as rock stars, and for a while as former rock stars, the Boys were as well- and ill-prepared for the era's changes as were their fans.

That made them suspect as has-beens until they regained their hip credentials. Then when times changed again, and for economic or political or musical or psychological reasons the Sixties came to an end, all their creative live and recorded music after *Pet Sounds* was a window that had been left open for their careers to continue far into the future, whether the Mike Love, Bruce Johnston "Kokomo" future, or the Brian, Al, Blondie, Wondermints, *Smile* future.

Through that window, hip was the stage after irony, which was the stage after defensiveness. On *Beach Boys' Party!* they are defensive when they let Al sing "The Times They Are A-Changin'" and then undercut him with their crowd noise, erecting a distance, so to speak, from acoustic-political Bob Dylan. They are ironic when they are goofing on their own oldie "Little Deuce

Coupe," acknowledging the distance they have traveled since then, but only by belittling their own past. They are hip with their affectionate engagement with their roots on "Barbara Ann." They can honor and make use of the distance to revitalize that old doo-wop hit.

Hip held the early and late '60s together, hip recognized the split in the decade, and hip accepted the changes in the world and the changes in the Beach Boys. Whether you think the Beach Boys achieved their version of hipness on *Smiley Smile*, as I do, or on *Surf's Up* or *The Beach Boys Love You*, or at the concert at Carnegie Hall, on the other side of that hip could be what the novelist Nelson Algren called an achieved innocence that comes through contact with the world.[1] And that's the earned innocence I believe led Brian to complete and release *Smile* thirty-seven years late, and to make it sound fresh.

11

The Best Unreleased Pop Album Ever

....

Like *Endless Summer* early '60s songs that fell from late '60s favor to return to even greater mid-'70s prominence, *Smile* moves forward and backward in time. Originally conceived for a 1967 release, with its "Surf's Up" track pre-hyped by no less than maestro Leonard Bernstein, *Smile* became a symbol of unmet '60s expectations by failing to materialize. Pieces leaked out from 1967 to 1971, polished up or refashioned on other Beach Boys albums: "Heroes and Villains," "Vegetables," "Wind Chimes," "Mama Says," "Our Prayer," "Cabinessence," and "Surf's Up." The 1967 *Smiley Smile* album, a brilliant stoner goof from the Beach Boys themselves,[1] was misperceived by *Rolling Stone* and others as the group's finished version of their masterwork. But if that album wasn't *Smile*, and it obviously wasn't, how did all the single pieces fit together? Or did they? Or would they ever?

Brian Wilson Presents Smile, completed in 2004 and presented in concert and on CD, was not the *Smile* that was never released in 1967, because those original pieces had never been assembled into a finalized, completed whole. Although the versions on the other albums appeared as separate songs, many of them were originally developed for *Smile* as themes that repeated through the record, just like, aw shucks, a real symphony, or as we used to call it, a rock opera. Brian, working with original *Smile* lyricist Van Dyke Parks and Darian Sahanaja from Brian's touring band, created the new *Brian Wilson Presents Smile* from the old pieces as assembled by historians and fans like Domenic Priore with additional lyrics and segues newly composed by Brian and Parks. This new *Smile* proved so successful that it was used as a template to arrange the original 1967 sessions and release them as *Smile: The Beach Boys* in 2011.

The 2011 version used the material recorded in 1967, so it featured those remarkably sweet yet powerful vocals from Brian and Carl singing in their twenties. The 2004 version was all newly recorded (in the same old studios) with harmonies from Brian's new younger band, alongside Brian's older, less supple vocals, a part of the music's multi-year patina, Carl having passed away in 1998.

As numerous Beach Boys session outtake releases reveal, Brian's music without the vocals isn't less of something but rather something different, and you get more of those so-called instrumental backing tracks on the 2011 Beach Boys version. Nonetheless, the addition of the missing vocals and lyrics on the 2004 Brian Wilson version of "Roll Plymouth Rock," "On a Holiday," and "Blue Hawaii," as well as other judicious lyrical and musical links, give *Brian Wilson Presents Smile* a more satisfying focus and flow. Maybe it's the 2004 perspective. Whatever—it works, and it invites us to hear this entire forty-seven-minute version of *Smile* as one interlocking composition.

One of the remarkable legacies of *Smile*'s thirty-seven-year disappearance is the belief that if the original could have been completed and released in 1967, it would have corrected much that went wrong with the counterculture, the nation, and even some fans' personal lives. Its very absence was a pop event. That's the psychological conceit explored in Lewis Shiner's 1993 novel *Glimpses*, whose protagonist, an unhappy stereo repairman and pop music fan, stumbles into time-traveling powers that allow him to intervene and help complete lost classic rock master-pieces including *Smile*.[2]

I'm one of a different set of fans who appreciated *Smile*'s "re-placement," *Smiley Smile*, as a charming, hip poke in the eye at late '60s rock pretension that can stand on its own. Discover-ing, almost four decades later, that *Smile* is even better than we imagined adds another wonderful layer of convolution to the Beach Boys saga. The goof or spoof or parodic take-off *Smiley Smile* appeared before the original *Smile*, and both are great. But no matter how you understand the gap, the thirty-seven-year dis-appearance is the context in which most people approach this music, and was the obvious opening for all the rave reviews that greeted *Smile*'s completion, including mine.[3]

The Beach Boys' penchant for sliding around inside their own chronology stretches back at least to *Beach Boys' Party!* in 1965. That record successfully mixed origin tributes like "Hully Gully" and "Devoted to You" with Beatles covers like "Tell Me Why," mash-ups of their own old car songs, and the surprise smash unplugged take on the Regents' doo-wop "Barbara Ann." In the '70s the Boys released and performed new material, while coming to terms with the new success of their own rereleased old *Endless Summer* hits. The *Love and Mercy* movie captures this jumbled chronology by cutting back and forth between Paul Dano's and John Cusack's portrayals of Brian Wilson in different decades. While the scram-

bled time frames—the newer 2011 Beach Boys version was actually recorded decades before the 2004 Brian Wilson older version
—proved those '60s anticipations were worth completing, they
also proved those anticipations were going to continue shifting
around inside the culture, rarely in a clear progression.

In both versions, *Smile* itself echoes this jumbled history with
its own nonlinear structure. We return again to themes of love
and innocence from *Pet Sounds*, but not through that album's
personal subjectivity. Now we are listening to a wider soundscape, guided by a more impersonal and more confident nar-
rator through America from Plymouth Rock to Hawaii, with
Indians, cowboys, Chinese laborers on the railroads, and a family farm. Occasional clear phrases bubble up from the hard-to-
follow lyrics and trade off with jingle-like vignettes as the big
picture scales down to hearing wind chimes and then scales
back up again. The movement is sometimes geographical and
sometimes historic, from east to west, from the Pilgrims landing
to a present-day vacation in Hawaii. But often the musical flow
disrupts these logical progressions, and provides connections
closer to a fairy tale or dream.

The centerpiece belongs to "Surf's Up," the public introduction to *Smile* in 1967, and the album's most ambitious and beautiful track. The first two-thirds or so of this song's evocative lyrics
aren't really undecipherable—if you want to pore over the clues
and interviews, you can decipher what they are "about." I believe, however, that the meanings are hard to figure out because
Brian and Van Dyke Parks didn't know exactly what they were
about themselves. Let's just say we hear references to an unde-
fined past with suggestions of a this-too-shall-pass premonition

and no clear references to the American locations or American events or American instrumentation scattered through the rest of the record. These lyrics ride the music and allow the lead singer to hit that high, heartbreaking falsetto on the final syllable of "domino" twice, mirroring the same syllable on *Pet Sounds*' "Caroline No," the last human syllable on that earlier album. It's not the last human syllable here. The lyrics simplify on the final third of "Surf's Up," the instrumentation settles down to some piano chords and a bass, and we finally hear the words in the title and return once again to an appeal for childlike innocence and faith.

But that's in the middle of the album. This *Smile* moves on, building to the "Mrs. O'Leary's Cow" Chicago Fire sequence, which, as the well-known story goes, was the bad vibes section that brought the original 1967 *Smile* sessions to chaos in the studio, pushed Brian over the edge, and probably derailed the entire project. Surviving the completion of that segment this time around on record and in live performance, Brian concludes with "In Blue Hawaii," a bit of "Our Prayer," and an early version of "Good Vibrations."

Hearing the songs in this order, and listening to the new wordplay that doesn't appear on the 1967–2011 version, I think it's clear that Brian, Van Dyke, and Darian are signaling that they know this is the biggest question *Smile* has to answer: Has it been finished, is it complete? That answer can't come until they get through the Chicago Fire. They do, so finished it is.

That leads to a second question: Is it any good? I love "Surf's Up" as a single track, but had *Smile* turned out to be an entire album of breathtaking, weighty music with frequently incomprehensible lyrics, it would have been a disappointment, proof that the Sixties was doomed to collapse under the weight of our weighty expectations. But the poetical parts of *Smile* are cut with the goofy, the slow with the perky, all tied together with Brian in high gear using his gift for chord changes that shouldn't work but do, and turning to his advantage his late-career propensity for creating song fragments rather than whole songs.

That leaves a third and final question: Is the whole of *Smile* really about anything other than being finished? I say yes. It's about America in 1967 as reimagined and clarified in 2004.

The Vietnam War years made many of us think about American invasions. At the same time, the collapse of JFK's New Frontier, the rise of California as the most populous state, and even the entrance of Hawaii as the fiftieth state presented a conclusion to the crossing aka settling aka conquest of the continent. Surfers flew to Hawaii to surf, and for the most part, flew back. There was no longer an empty space further west to fill up with an internal mass migration. Maybe this is not as firmly lodged in our unconscious now as it was in 1967. Back then, we were only two generations away from eradicating the Native Americans in California,[4] and just finishing up the '50s with westerns on TV and in the movies. Those images and most of the cowboy music connected to them came out of Hollywood, but took place and were usually shot on the other, eastern side of the mountains, as if the national imagination was still pondering that portion of our history and hadn't yet made it to the coast. The '60s followed those images of cowboys on the desert with images of surfers on the California coastline—one of surfing's deepest unconscious connections—as Americans realized that our civilization had finally settled into our western border. Now what? Paddle out, surf back, repeat. Or spill over into Vietnam.

Smile doesn't try to organize a sequential narrative, but it does toss out a lot of interconnecting themes and images. These allow a listener to hear the arrival of Europeans at Plymouth Rock as the origin of the destruction of the sacred lands of Native Americans, replaced by our rural past, replaced by iron railroads, and then, by implication, concrete highways. I hear that in the lyrics as I understand them. Am I reading all that into the music? Maybe so. But the music is composed and arranged to invite such a reading into.

If *Pet Sounds* can be heard as a struggle to maintain the innocence of romantic love and commitment, the innocence necessary to create some great pop music, then *Smile*, scattering phrases about faith and belief through very American sounds, references, and images, can be heard as a struggle to maintain faith in America itself, or even in faith itself. But why is that a struggle?

Unlike *Pet Sounds*, *Smile* is essentially energetic music, and it's possible to make the case that it's a celebration of America, or one version of America. Michael Anton pulls this off in his "Paradise Lost and Regained"[5] from the Spring 2012 issue of the *Claremont Review*, the conservative counterpart to the *New York Review of Books*. Anton favors the 2011 Beach Boys version of *Smile*, which works with his perspective: it's the version with the prettier, younger Wilson brothers' vocals, and without the additional clarifying lyrics about American Indians. Anton's conservative claim places Brian's optimism in opposition to the late anti-Americanism of the New Left.

Tom Smucker

This claim contains the fun-in-the-sun fallacy, a misperception or misrepresentation that the Beach Boys' music was upbeat until it had to confront late '60s negativity. But their downbeat edge colors their music going all the way back to "Lonely Sea" on their second album, or even "County Fair" and "Heads You Win, Tails I Lose" on the first album, and all the way through *Smile* up to *No Pier Pressure*. In fact, it is those gloomy undercurrents, combined with their optimism, that give their early music its lasting depth. Raised to not rock the boat, the Boys grew up in a culture I also experienced when I was growing up, one that masked but could not eliminate confusion, pain, and anger. That norm made it harder for the group to signal their turn to more complex and nuanced art, and often made it harder for them to accept all the complex emotions their own music was uncovering and expressing.

The Beach Boys had arrived at pop prominence as representatives of a new social reality, a mass suburban prosperity less stable and more racist than it needed to be or liked to acknowledge. When the times required pop music that reflected the abrupt social and personal disruptions forced on young men and their friends and families by the Vietnam War, the Beach Boys were obligated to respond. They had to change with that changing reality or disappear.

That did not require them to become political activists, or to turn against whatever was fun and wonderful about America, Southern California in the early '60s, lower-middle-class suburbia, and their own lives. But it did require music that one way or another engaged with the struggle over what was worth saving from the past and how to save it. In their *Endless Summer* songs, the Beach Boys distilled and captured much of what was best about postwar American prosperity, and how they shepherded that distillation through the Vietnam War years and beyond was important. Figuring out what was best, of course, implies also figuring out what was not.

When we finally heard it, *Smile* was indeed addressing this big picture, and addressing it in Brian Wilson–Beach Boys fashion. By then, the decades long gap was a part of the music's social context, as was the story that recording the Chicago Fire sequence in *Smile* scared its creator. Whatever the private reality may have been, the idea that the great intuitive genius of white American Sixties pop was frightened by his own creation and slept through much of the next decade resonates for many of us who shared that time and space, and it has become a part of the mythology of the era for those born later. And this idea links to the not-always-acknowledged negative undercurrents that were an important component of the Beach Boys' appeal from the beginning, and which became an enduring part of their appeal in the end. If Brian couldn't finish *Smile* for thirty-seven years, this validates the idea that the ambitions and disruptions of the late '60s were indeed that powerful and painful. And if he could only finish it in the recent past, but indeed could finish it, this validates the idea that we can still fashion a hard, ambitious, complex American faith, and need to.

The Vietnam War is a ghost floating through the late '60s and early '70s, and still floating through our consciousness today. How each of us deals with that ghost may differ, but noticing that ghost isn't "politically correct." It's politically realistic, honoring all the emotions and life changes connected to that freakishly ever-altering war. Recalling how Vietnam raised the issue of our having layered a new civilization on top of the one already in place for Native Americans isn't pretentious or un-American. It's what happened. The album cover of 1971's *Surf's Up* depicts the *End of the Trail* statue. Juxtaposing an exhausted Native American brave on a horse with the group's first album title to mention surf since *Surfer Girl* may have been heartfelt or opportunistic or both. But it fit the times and was an accurate advertisement for the album's ambitions, whether you feel it achieved those ambitions or did not. If this was calculated, it was no more so than the cover of *Surfer Girl* or *Shut Down Vol. 2*.

In the documentary *Beautiful Dreamer: Brian Wilson and the Story of Smile*,[6] we get to see Brian completing and performing *Smile* after over an hour of history and context establishing the demons he confronted with his performance. By then, this personal, musical, and social context feels overpowering. As I sat in my living room watching the DVD for the first time in years, the ovation from the London audience after the 2004 debut jerked my real tears once again. For Brian, for the Beach Boys, for myself, for the last fifty years.

12

The Beatles

....

The cliché was true. After Kennedy's assassination, and the assassination of his alleged assassin, the United States needed some kind of good news. And here came those clever, upbeat Brits, playing a hand no American pop group had been dealt. Besides being geniuses, the Beatles liked our music so much they wanted in on it, and that was comforting. At the same time, the Beatles could appreciate, absorb, and borrow from all our pop rock without getting stuck inside any of our regional, ethnic, musical, or political divisions, and that was a relief. They could act enthusiastic about the States, and that was refreshing. Yet because they also sounded and looked like they were from someplace else, and knew it, the Beatles were both innocent and hip. They created the greatest American cultural achievement of the American century because they weren't Americans.

If Brian Wilson had been the well-adjusted, productive Paul McCartney of Hawthorne, maybe the Beach Boys would have evolved like the Beatles. He wasn't, they didn't, and I don't think the times made it possible. Michael Jackson and Prince came close for a while—stories that deserve their own books, but point toward a similar conclusion. There couldn't have been an American Beatles. No American could have been that American.

No American could have escaped being someone from somewhere. No American could have claimed that kind of innocence. And the Beatles couldn't claim it forever.

The evidence of their influence first surfaced on *Beach Boys' Party!*, which slid two current Beatles tunes ("I Should Have Known Better" and "Tell Me Why") in with the oldies. From *Rubber Soul* to *Pet Sounds* to *Sgt. Pepper*, and maybe *Revolver* to *Smile*, the Beach Boys and the Beatles were listening to, but not imitating, each other's records. But though they may have borrowed each other's ideas, they didn't borrow each other's vibes. *Rubber Soul* is where clever goes pensive, while *Pet Sounds* is emotional, often downright unhappy. *Sgt. Pepper* is confident, clever, perky, and ends on profound. Thirty-seven years later, *Smile* is profound, yet also goofy—more Mark Twain than Jane Austen. Could it have been the American *Sgt. Pepper*?

No. *Smile* could not have sounded as confident as the Beatles did in 1967. No American music could have. That's one reason it was so hard to complete. The expectation that the album was supposed to fulfill was impossible. *Smile* sounded better getting released in 2004 because it only had to be complete and really good to be amazing. The Beatles got there first—they got to be amazing first, and you can't top that kind of amazing. The Beatles themselves never did. By the time the White Album was released, they realized they would have to break up.

13

Into the Genres

....

In their more than five decades, Beach Boys songs have inspired remarkably few successful cover versions. Here are some worthwhile exceptions and notable failures.

Disco

L.A. (Light Album), from 1979, included the Beach Boys' disastrous ten-minute disco version of *Wild Honey*'s "Here Comes the Night." Guitar-based instrumental surf music lent itself to disco do-overs, but classic Beach Boys harmony pop was too tightly structured to stretch out, not designed to slowly build to a climax. On top of that, much of the group's audience was hardening into ominous, reactionary, disco-sucks rockers. Booed when it debuted in concert, the disco "Here Comes the Night" was quickly retired. The closest that one of their tunes ever came to a functional disco version cover was on the authentic-for-the-era nonexistent group Good Vibrations' "Don't Worry Baby," on their eponymous 1978 Millennium/Casablanca album (with Luther Vandross in the credits!). The track eliminated all references to drag races or really anything but the title: seven minutes and twenty seconds of obscure but authentic disco. The LP's other four attempts to drag the Beach Boys onto that kind of dance floor were flops. Disco was a better fit for a Four Seasons song. The Seasons' 1966 hit "Working My Way Back to You" returned to the pop, r&b, and dance charts in 1979 as one-half of a Spinners' hit medley.

Country

The Beach Boys: Stars and Stripes Vol. 1, a 1996 collaboration with Nashville celebrities, sounded like it was aimed at a double crossover of the Beach Boys in their America's Band mode with suburbanizing, patriotic, rocking country, but it was conservative in the worst way—boring—and never led to a follow-up. The Beach Boys' vocal roots weren't country; they came out of doo-wop and pop jazz, not the southern white gospel of the Jordanaires. But there were spaces that could have been explored in the shared territory of white guilt and loneliness when the America's Band baloney was dropped. Willie Nelson finds it on *Stars and Stripes* with "Warmth of the Sun," and Brian Wilson and Tammy Wynette's duet on "In My Room" from 1998's *Tammy Wynette Remembered* is absolutely hair-raising. Wynette finds the terror in the dark as well as the comfort inside the song's isolation on what was probably her last recording. She was only fifty-five when she passed away. The other successful country venture was also a Brian duet, in 2015 with Kacey Musgraves on *No Pier Pressure*'s "Guess You Had to Be There." And let's add a kind word about the road not taken beyond 2005's inventive *Pickin' on the Beach Boys: A Bluegrass Tribute*, with Mike Toppins on dobro and banjo. His "Help Me Rhonda" clears one's mind of all the bad covers out there, and proves the connection between the compressed Scruggs picking energy packed inside the formal constraints of bluegrass and the compressed energy packed inside the Beach Boys' tightly structured classic rockers, leading us all back once again to Chuck Berry.

Punk

The Beach Boys catalog lends itself more to power-pop than punk. It doesn't have much to offer those loaded up on just three chords and a lot of attitude. Longtime Pittsburgh garage rockers the Cynics break on through on "Be True to Your School," a highlight of 1990's *Smiles, Vibes, & Harmony: A Tribute to Brian Wilson*. Michael Kastelic's vocals push the simple-minded yet profound lyrics past tribute and parody to uncover the real punk heart of the song, making this not just a cover, but an improvement.

Jazz

"Caroline No" and "God Only Knows" may yet become jazz standards, and as long as there's a Bill Frisell, we can never give up hope that he might find more. A man who can situate covers from my two musical heroes—Brian Wilson's "Surfer Girl" and Junior Wells's "Messin' with the Kid"—next to each other on *Guitar in the Space Age!* (OKeh) can yet achieve anything. In the meantime, the only full-length jazz release so far is 1997's *Wouldn't It Be Nice: A Jazz Portrait of Brian Wilson*, produced by Tim Weston, with contributions from Larry Carlton, the Yellowjackets, and others. Most interesting are the bits from the a capella Clark Burroughs Group. Burroughs was the high tenor in the Hi-Los, the Brian Wilson, so to speak, of the other big late '50s and early '60s white pop jazz vocal quartet besides the Four Freshmen. As part of an authentic jazz influence on Brian, Burroughs's contributions suggest where Beach Boys' vocals might have traveled without rock and roll.

Indie-Alt Rock

Portland Smiles, a charming and hilarious digital-only cover of *Smiley Smile* from a diverse crew rounded up on Portland's Tender Loving Empire label, is so perfect it makes you believe that after failing to release *Smile*, the Beach Boys invented alt and indie rock, if not the city of Portland itself. Using a different artist or group on each cut fits *Smiley Smile*'s patchwork flow and pulls the two big hits, "Heroes and Villains" and "Good Vibrations," down into the digital stream, rather than astride the tops of the original two vinyl sides. Since all participants share a quirky Portland sensibility, I rate this not as a cover version or a tribute, but as an improvement that makes the original sound even better.

If nothing else, *Portland Smile* proves that the albums the Beach Boys released after *Pet Sounds*, after *Smile* was abandoned, were creative, not dysfunctional, and opened up new options for pop music without closing down any of the old ones.

And Beyond

Here are five really great cover versions that didn't fit anywhere else in the book but deserve some recognition.

"Add Some Music to Your Day," Kate Campbell, from *Making God Smile*. A Dolly Partonish, clear-headed folkie reading with good diction and tasteful acoustic guitar brings out all the charm in a charming *Sunflower* track that was trying too hard to become a hit single.

"Girl Don't Tell Me," Vivian Girls, from the seven-inch *Surf's Up*. Here's a lovely punky queering of the *Endless Summer* track.

"In My Room," Linda Ronstadt, from *Dedicated to the One I Love*. This example of Ronstadt's lullabizing of rock standards is almost as good as her "We Will Rock You."

"Sail On Sailor," Jamie Cullum with Fred Martin and the Levite Camp, from the *Musicares Presents a Tribute to Brian Wilson* DVD. Cullum and the gospel choir unlock the Pentecost hiding in this hit by pushing it past mere rocking. Tongues of fire.

"A Day in the Life of a Tree," Suzy and Maggie Roche, from *Why the Long Face*. One of Brian's most peculiar and most touching songs gets some love from two-thirds of those clever sisters, who know how to make eccentric seem to be just the way things are.

14

Dennis

....

The middle Wilson brother: the only real surfer, the sex symbol, the drummer; the Beach Boy who got entangled with Charles Manson, supported Brian's projects, did drugs with Brian, slept with Mike's wife, composed some classic Beach Boys songs, released a solo album, drowned at age thirty-nine in the waters off Marina Del Rey, committed suicide by alcohol, and was buried at sea with a special civilian dispensation from President Reagan.

Someone had to be the real surfer. Someone had to be the drummer.

When he wanted to, Dennis could cut to the heart of the classic Beach Boys themes of romantic and erotic anxiety and reassurance with his contributions "Cuddle Up" and "Forever." His raspy-voiced, Wagnerian, white soul solo album, 1977's *Pacific Ocean Blue*, was a surprise—an acquired taste I never acquired, climbing too far for me from the confessional to the operatic on tracks that I felt could use some editing. But the drummer had found his own voice. He had and has a following, a noteworthy elaboration on the meaning of the Beach Boys, and the strongest of any of the group's solo albums, if you don't count *Smile*.

But Dennis could never settle into a truce between his desires and his needs. He was swept away by the rock-and-roll life, the counterculture, and the family demons. His involvement with mass murderer Charles Manson was more than a one-night miscalculation. Manson and his followers moved in with Dennis, providing sex and drugs, and apparently expected a record contract for Manson, which was not forthcoming and probably led to the Manson-orchestrated murders. It was a long and nearly fatal engagement with a demonic mutation of patriarchy, Manson's homicidal mix of Beatle worship, ersatz spirituality, and heterosexual sex on demand, whose side effects were a lot worse than mere gonorrhea.[1] It could easily have been Dennis, his family, his frequent collaborator Terry Melcher, or really any of the Beach Boys murdered that night instead of the Beach Boys' hair stylist Jay Sebring, along with Sharon Tate. Less circumspect than Carl about sharing his opinions with the media, Dennis never answered a question or said anything in public about the Manson family after they were arrested.

Dennis resonates for many of us who lived through those times as the good-looking but regular guy who got caught up in the changes and didn't have the ego strength or good luck or judgment or stability to turn away in time from the many big and little Mansons who were engendered by the counterculture in the later '60s.

If the Beach Boys had been able to communicate and collaborate into the late '70s and early '80s, if Dennis could have found a way to deal directly with the Manson trauma, and if the three Wilson brothers had not each in turn gone down their rabbit holes of heroin, cocaine, and booze, then maybe Dennis could have channeled his creativity and his hot mess of emotions into the group or a solo career. Instead, he struggled and failed to complete *Bambu*, the follow-up to *Pacific Ocean Blue*. When Carl backed out of their co-owned studio, Dennis had to sell his share to pay off debts, and the downward spiral continued. He drowned five years later. Learning from your older brother how to compose using the recording studio as an instrument is no longer helpful when that instrument has been sold.

In movies from concerts and in TV shows of the early years, Dennis has a sexy, distracted onstage look that strikes me as a variation on Brian's anxious look, as if they're both not quite convinced they want to be there, as if they're not sure they are really pleasing their dad, or want to. At the beginning, that look was a part of Dennis's charm—the hot average guy, lucky to be Brian Wilson's brother and happy to be in the band. In the end, it wasn't enough.

15

Carl

....

When Brian quit touring, his youngest brother Carl became the musical director for the concerts, while Mike continued as emcee. Carl's singing and playing were at the heart of the Beach Boys' early 1970s shows, when they were building toward their comeback and at their peak as a versatile, tight, confident live band. As Brian withdrew from the studio, Carl took over most of the production as well. A purer and more versatile Brian on the vocals, Carl also mimicked Brian's production style on many of the group's early '70s recordings. His stunning 1969 cover of the Ronettes' "I Can Hear Music" on the 20/20 album was a brilliant reimagining of Brian improving on Phil Spector, with Carl one-upping Brian's vocals. Carl's perfect pitch, range, and well-preserved voice, along with his skill at translating recordings to live performances, maintained a continuity of sound for a group with a fractious personality. His tinkering, barely behind the scenes, salvaged more than one Brian Is Back release when Brian wasn't really back.

Blessed or cursed with a placid response to his own abbreviated childhood—he was in a famous rock band by the time he was fifteen—Carl is usually mentioned in Beach Boys history as a character in someone else's story. He's the son who didn't have a fight with Murry; was hardly starring role material for a made-for-TV movie; and was the subject of only one biography,[1] a good one by surf music historian Kent Crowley. Even in Crowley's book, it's hard to pry Carl's story away from the story of Brian Wilson and the Beach Boys. He's the Beach Boy included in the sessions when Brian started using the Wrecking Crew professionals in the studio, Brian's trusted double-check, the only Beach Boy besides Brian playing an instrument on *Pet Sounds*, and the Beach Boy who could actually duplicate Chuck Berry's "Johnny B. Goode" riff.

The Japanese compilation CD *I Can Hear Music: The Beach Boys Lead Vocal by Carl Wilson* contains twenty-two tracks, from "Wild Honey" to "Good Vibrations" to "Palisades Park." Few are remembered by the public as Carl Wilson solos. Conversely, because he covered all of Brian's vocals in the live shows for many decades, regular fans remember Carl's singing, not Brian's, on "Caroline No" and "Surf's Up." These became Carl's songs in concert, further fudging his vocal identity with his brother's. As a fan in the early '70s when Brian wasn't touring, when the live band was cooking in concert and Carl was writing and performing his new music, I understood Carl to be the center of the Beach Boys, with Mike as the humorous emcee, Dennis as the smoldering sex symbol, and Al as Al.

Carl's first two compositions on a Beach Boys album surfaced on 1971's *Surf's Up*, and his production and vocal overdubs reclaimed that crucial title track. After "Trader" on 1973's *Holland*, I'm partial to "Full Sail" from the Beach Boys' 1979 *L.A. (Light Album)*, "Heaven" from the 1981 solo *Carl Wilson* album, and "Of the Times" from Carl's 1983 solo *Youngblood*. But none of these late '70s or early '80s tracks pack the spiritual or pop oomph Carl was capable of creating in the late '60s and early '70s.

Memoirs and bios mention Carl's late '70s hard-drug-induced near catastrophes on tour in Australia and in New York's Central Park, the divorce from Annie, moving to his mountain home in Colorado, debilitating back pain, and his early '80s solo career that never quite took flight. But all his turmoil was overshadowed by the drama of Brian's withdrawal and his unscrupulous therapist, Dennis's near-death interactions with Charles Manson, and Mike's multiple marriages and divorces. For better and for worse, Carl remained fixed in public consciousness as the quiet brother.

His one great late-career impact was his falsetto hook on 1988's "Kokomo," stamping that million-selling US number one hit as undeniably the Beach Boys. By that point, Carl was the only functioning member capable of replicating that gorgeous portion of their trademark sound. But it would remain a one-hit exclamation point, not a new departure for the group. As the tours moved ever closer to recycling old hits, there was ever less space for exploring new material, including Carl's.

An oldest-youngest brother drama lies below the surface of the public stories, but there are few hints of that tension or affection or estrangement in the music. Carl died in 1998 from metastasized lung cancer. He'd been smoking cigarettes since he was thirteen, although miraculously, it had never seemed to affect his voice. With his passing, the Beach Boys effectively ended as a real group. There would be the 50th anniversary tour, and Mike and Bruce would tour with the contractual rights to use the Beach Boys name, but Carl had been the core and he was gone.

16

Al, Bruce, and David

....

Al Jardine's got the voice that blends in, and over the years, he's blended in with different Beach Boys factions. Sometimes he was in the healthy living, anti-druggie Transcendental Meditation faction with Mike and Bruce; sometimes he was touring off on his own; sometimes he was with his sons and Brian and Marilyn's daughters Wendy and Carnie, two-thirds of the group Wilson Phillips. As I write, Al is touring with Brian and his band, with his own son Matt handling the falsettos. Of the original Beach Boys who are still alive, only Al still sounds like his younger self.

Al was the folk singer, the original Kingston Trio fan. On 1965's *Beach Boys Party!* he sang an acoustic cover of Dylan's "The Times They Are A-Changin'," a good folkie fit with the forward-backward time frame of that album. It's always seemed simultaneously appropriate and upsetting that the crowd on that party album lets Al sing but alternates shouting out "right!" and then "wrong!" after each line of the song, satirizing or maybe just fucking with Al. I could identify with being the sincere folkie at that kind of party with those kinds of comments when I was still in high school, a strain of Beach Boys authenticity that did not induce nostalgia.

In 2015, when Capitol released *Beach Boys' Party! Uncovered and Unplugged*, a two-CD set of all the original album's session takes minus the fake-live party sounds, I was amazed to find the "right!" and "wrong!" chants had disappeared. They were not in the studio chatter. They had been recorded and added later. We could finally hear Al do Dylan straight up. Why was that the only song on the record screwed around with in that way? Which part of changin' times was that party trying to dismiss?

....

When Bruce Johnston was added to the group after Brian quit touring, he was already a music industry insider with his own career in surf and hot rod music. Fitting easily into the Beach Boys' vocal harmony blend, Bruce also had the ability to write songs in Brian's style, if perhaps a little sweeter. Still, if you weren't paying close attention, his contributions helped add continuity through some of the struggles after *Pet Sounds*. Johnston's "The Nearest Faraway Place" on *20/20* could have been one of Brian's instrumentals. His "Deirdre" and "Tears in the Morning" fit right into *Sunflower*'s vibe. On 1971's *Surf's Up*, Johnston stepped into his own identity with "Disney Girls (1957)," a perfectly executed wistful wish list for escaping the '60s, a bourgeois companion to Merle Haggard's "Okie From Muskogee." When I first heard the song on the LP, I was enthralled and still am. When I heard Johnston debut it with the Beach Boys back in the day at Princeton University, and the audience broke into cheers over the line about renouncing reality, I freaked. Winsome recollection is one thing, reactionary willfulness another. A good fit with *Surf's Up*'s progressive nostalgia, "Disney Girls (1957)" is still performed by

Bruce on tour with Mike and their version of the Beach Boys. But the song has lost much of its mellow power. Maybe those imaginary '50s are too far away for a concert that puts its energy into reviving the early '60s. Or maybe much of the Beach Boys' audience has actually returned to the fantasy world of 1957 since that song was first performed. If so, that's scary.

Bringing David Marks back as a part of the Beach Boys 50th anniversary tour seemed like stretching it. He hadn't been in the group for decades. But hey, he's the fifth Beach Boy on the covers of the first four albums, a talented guitar player with a current retro surf music album called *Back to the Garage*; and he's the kid who grew up across the street from the Wilsons in Hawthorne, traded guitar chops with Carl when they were both in the band, and continued to commute with Carl to Hollywood Professional High School after he left/got kicked out of the group. A close look at the early history shows all sorts of combinations of Brian, Al, and David in the live concert lineup. He's an interesting interviewee when they get him into the documentaries, and with Carl and Dennis gone, he's the youngest member left alive from those earliest tours and recordings, the only human link to a single year when two suburban neighbors just beginning high school turned into rock stars.

17

Mike

....

One recent springtime evening in Kansas, I caught a well-performed, audience-pleasing double-bill concert of the Temptations and the Beach Boys. Of the dozen or more members from both groups on the stage, Mike Love was the only original. Putting authenticity issues aside, Mike pays for the contractual rights to tour as the Beach Boys. Brian chooses to tour as himself, even when he sometimes outnumbers Mike in former Beach Boys onstage, and even if they both play a lot of the same classic hits and both close with "Barbara Ann" and "Fun, Fun, Fun."

The videos at these recent Beach Boys concerts show old clips of the group in their striped shirts, as surfers, as hippies, with the Beatles and the Maharishi, performing for an audience of half a million at the Washington Mall. At times, a younger Mike Love on the screen lip-synchs a duet with the old Mike Love onstage. Some might find this pathetic, but the audiences like it, and I think it's fascinating.

A few years ago, these Beach Boys led by Mike Love were touring without any videos or props, claiming that the audience should be allowed to let the music evoke individual, personal memories—Mike's "sonic oasis" theory. Now as Mike fronts these concerts, he sketches the history of the group, shading it toward his own contributions, of course, but not shying away from recognizing Brian's, including *Pet Sounds*, or those of Carl and Dennis. Onstage, in his memoir *Good Vibrations: My Life as a Beach Boy*, in interviews, and in documentaries, Mike works to portray the Beach Boys as a group with a history that participates in history.

Mike's the Beach Boy who's worked the hardest to puzzle out how and where they can position themselves in the current moment, and where they fit into the past. Whether that's savvy marketing or historical perspective, it impels an awareness of surroundings, attention to social context. When the group was forming, Mike was newly married, with a baby, pumping gas. Brian may have had the internal artistic inspiration. Mike needed a better job.

In the early 1980s, the Beach Boys were in a slump when the newly ascendant Reagan administration threw them an accidental PR bonanza. Far, far right oil-drilling zealot Interior Secretary James Watt banned the Boys from performing free at the Washington Mall on the Fourth of July because they would attract "the wrong element," and invited Las Vegas fixture and bona fide Republican Wayne Newton instead. Transformed overnight from going-over-the-hill wimps to controversial bad asses, the Beach Boys, largely navigated by Mike, parlayed this dis into an invitation to meet the first family in the White House and host the Fourth on the Mall the following year with America, the O'Jays, Hank Williams Jr., La Toya Jackson, and an audience of half a million. A happy outcome, but let's remember, President Reagan appointed Watt and would have let him get away with banning the Beach Boys if the publicity had not been so unforgiving.

Keeping this story inside the history of the group obviously elevates Mike's importance, but it's a great story that also re-inserts the history of the group inside the history of the country, hence Mike's branding of the Beach Boys as America's Band. You can take that as a positive, post–James Watt affirmation of diversity and optimism; or as confirmation that a group of talented, troubled, quarreling, often drug addicted, well-intentioned, at times dysfunctional white musicians from Southern California did indeed qualify in the Reagan years as America's Band. Or you can take it as a white-heads-in-the-sand retreat to an early '60s that never existed.

Mike's Beach Boys weave together patriotism, nostalgia, and environmentalism as their legacy. But as I write, politicians, right-wing populist pundits, and corporate-funded ideologues are working to pry off and discard environmentalism while tightening the bond between patriotism and nostalgia. In formation we can glimpse a lethal patriotic nostalgia for a world of white supremacy, dirty water, and polluted beaches.

In histories of the Beach Boys, it's usually overlooked that Mike was the cousin who did not go to Hawthorne High School, or to hipster Uni High with the West LA, affluent cool kids like Jan and Dean and Bruce Johnston and Kim Fowley. He went to multiracial Dorsey High, and heard blues and doo-wop in the locker room and on the track field, not just on the radio. (The first line in "Help Me Rhonda" is African American slang Mike picked up at school, "out doin' in my head."[1]) And Mike, as far as I can tell, was the only white rocker back in the day who penned lyrics about the white students gunned down at Kent State in May, 1970, and also included the black students gunned down at Jackson State that same month ("Student Demonstration Time").[2] I can't think of another white band from the early '60s similar to the Beach Boys that tours with black groups like the Temptations.

Let's hope Mike stays engaged with his stage act and his legacy long enough to steer Beach Boys history through this ominous new era. Conditions are changing once again that will affect the marketing of a pop music act more than fifty years old. Mike may not be the Picasso of the Beach Boys, but he's the one most in touch with some American contradictions in desperate need of positive resolutions.

Mike's late-2017 double CD *Unleash the Love* highlights his Eastern Indian spirituality toward the end of the first disc. (The second features new versions of old Beach Boys songs.) Forty years ago, tracks like "10,000 Years Ago" about evolving toward world peace, or name-dropping Marvin Gaye on "Make Love, Not War" would have sounded like obvious attempts to hop on a hippie pop bandwagon. These days, they contain a bit of anti-nationalistic, career-threatening bravado. It will be interesting to see if these songs make it into Mike's live shows and limit his regular invitations to perform at the White House.

18

Brian Solo

....

Beginning with 1988's *Brian Wilson*, he's been a solo act longer than he was a Beach Boy, releasing fifteen albums, including two live concert LPs, two collaborations, ten solo LPs, 2017's *Playback* compilation, and Brian's contributions to 2012's Beach Boys 50th anniversary reunion LP. Like some artists from the Sixties, Brian could have returned to in-person performing on the cheap. But his touring band consists of the same brilliant Brian acolytes who first helped reproduce *Pet Sounds* live, and then helped complete, perform, and record *Smile*, from the LA power-pop Wondermints—Darian Sahanaja, Nick Walusko, Mike D'Amico, and Probyn Gregory—and Chicago connections through Brian's frequent co-producer Joe Thomas. Given Brian's reputation as a reclusive studio genius, the second-biggest story of his solo career after *Smile* has been his extensive, consistent touring, keeping him in the public eye. In that sense, he isn't exactly a solo act. You attend his concerts expecting his wonderful Wondermints-based band as well.

There are worthwhile cuts on all of Brian's solo recordings, including some Brian-style oddball songs. But none of the other newer albums can deliver *Smile*'s punch. How could they?

The first is among the strongest. *Brian Wilson* placed the

most tracks on *Playback*—four. I find the production on that first album a bit too brittle, the vibe a bit too forced. Apparently Dr. Landy, on his first go-round as Brian's shrink, had to be prevented by Sire Records from ruining *Brian Wilson* with his own mix. Already blurring the distinction between psychotherapist and co-producer, Landy's meddling managed to kill off any interest in a follow-up album. *Brian Wilson* was reissued in 2000 on Warner Archives/Rhino with bonus cuts and Landy's name removed from all but one credit, inspiring another Brian what-if. Suppose that Brian had been in a position to build on his first album, continuing to work with those musicians, free from Landy or any other meddlers with misplaced ideas of how his music might be manipulated into a hit, and suppose that he had not withdrawn throughout the 1990s?

Of the live Brian Wilson releases, my favorite is the 2000 two-CD release *Live at the Roxy Theatre*. This is Brian at the crest of his comeback, returning to Los Angeles, playing the five-hundred-seat club. He's up, the crowd is up, and the two new songs included make it onto *Playback*. Of the collaborations, I like 1995's *Orange Crate Art*, composed by Van Dyke Parks and sung by Brian Wilson, because it dares a little eccentricity and skips impossible ambitions for a hit. 1997's *The Wilsons* isn't really Brian working with his two grown-up daughters Wendy and Carly, two-thirds of Wilson Phillips. He guests on only three songs and wrote only one. But any sentimental parent who's a Beach Boys fan and remembers those daughters as little girls at live concerts, followed by all those years of public estrangement, has to cherish this CD, if only for the title and the photo on the back, and I'm one of those parents.

Three albums showcase Brian covering standards in three different genres: 2005's *What I Really Want for Christmas*, 2010's *Brian Wilson Reimagines Gershwin*, and 2011's *In the Key of Disney*. I agree with the selections on the *Playback* anthology. If you're familiar with Beach Boys music, this isn't going to surprise you. Each has its moments, each can also sound predictable, and none has Brian singing when he was in his twenties. Worth noting on the Gershwin CD: Brian's take on "I Loves You Porgy" and "It Ain't Necessarily So."

His older voice works well on *Smile*, marking the multi-year gap in completion, and works well on his driving-into-the-sunset trilogy that concludes the 50th anniversary *That's Why God Made the Radio* album. But his younger voice was more supple and expressive and able to blend into as well as stand out from the harmonies. That's why my favorite of his solo-era CDs is the most recent, 2015's *No Pier Pressure*. It allows Brian to compose for and sing with a variety of guest vocalists, both young and old, without having to carry the whole song on his end-of-career voice. On "Guess You Had to Be There" with young country star Kacey Musgraves, about both a wild night on the town and Brian's entire late '60s milieu and debacle, Kacey's vocals carry the song's bemused wisdom and innocence, and Brian only has to sound like himself. Freed from managing all the album's lead vocals on his own, Brian nails three of them, "This Beautiful Day," "The Last Song," and the song to his wife that plays over the *Love and Mercy* closing credit roll, "One Kind of Love."

In the end, the great subject of Brian's comeback career is Brian himself. And the essential point of each new release is the proof that he's alive and functioning and creating new music. Not all of it is profound or mind-blowing, but much of it is very good, and some of it captures a poignant power unique in rock-era pop. Devotees like me would appreciate Brian and his band shaping his post–Beach Boys musical output by playing more of it live in concert, working some new tunes into the set list the way the Beach Boys did in concert in the early '70s—the way Brian and his band have managed with "Love and Mercy," and the way they mix the new *No Pier Pressure* songs with the standards on the *Brian Wilson and Friends* DVD. *Playback*'s existence could help make that happen, but it opts for a little of this and a little of that, for highlights instead of a story. I believe *Smile* settled the issue of Brian being a genius, and revisiting *Smile* on *Playback* adds nothing new. The real ongoing story is Brian reflecting on his present and past, and *Playback* with some judicious editing could have pulled that story together from the last fifteen albums.

But the bulk of the audience is happy to hear the old standards. The prolonged *Pet Sounds* 50th anniversary tours were one way around this, making the whole album an oldie, allowing its lesser-known tracks nightly exposure. Unfortunately, the other albums' 50th anniversaries aren't getting similar treatments. Still, an old fan can dream of a Brian Wilson concert after intermission recreating all of *Smiley Smile*, or *Wild Honey*, or *Friends* or *20/20* or *Sunflower*. As the vaults open up and digitally stream the fifty-year-old outtakes from these sessions, pulling them back into the spotlight, maybe it will happen.

If nothing else, Brian's solo output, in concert and on recordings, makes it clear that *Smile* wasn't dusted off to revive a faltering career and juice a back catalog. It was completed and performed in a context of creativity and experimentation, by musicians and movers and shakers devoted to the music of Brian Wilson, including Brian himself.

19

Storytellers, Historians, and Fans

....

"The Beach Boys are hard to put into words," began the liner notes on one of their own Capitol albums, *Dance, Dance, Dance*, a trimmed, cheapo reissue of 1965's *Beach Boys Today!* The put-down continued into the next paragraph: "The Beach Boys do not offer a clear conception of the nature of man like, say, the Stones, nor like the Beatles, true images of themselves." And later, in the damning-with-faint-praise conclusion, "The Beach Boys' music had a vitality waves ahead of the standard brand of pre-acne pap prevalent in the early, pre-Beatles 60s." Dazzled by Brits, the liner notes didn't notice that the album they were on went Top 10 when first released in the United States and UK *after*, say, the Stones and the Beatles arrived in the States peddling their clear conceptions.

This was only one of the many low-water markers from the Beach Boys' late '60s slide. The group hadn't only gone out of fashion, it had nearly disappeared from comprehension. Those liner notes were close to true in only one sense: few people knew what to say.

The first substantial, successful attempt to fit the Beach Boys into prevailing ideas about rock music was Jules Siegel's "Goodbye Surfing, Hello God," in *Cheetah*, October 1967. By then, the

Boys were finished with their surf, car, and summer hits and had released *Pet Sounds* and "Good Vibrations." By then, Brian was struggling with *Smile*. The profile put the hook in its title, lumping together all the group's old music and contrasting that against the new music emerging from their hippie enlightenment. Siegel placed himself inside his story as a participant-observer sucked into the craziness and fun instigated by Brian, the genius eccentric, at home with his new retinue of hipsters, in the studio with the elite of LA pop musicians. The portrait hinged on the contrasts, not the continuity, in the Beach Boys' career.

When *Smile* was shelved and the group continued to release new music, this contrast unhinged. Whether the three albums that appeared in the year and a half after "Good Vibrations" —*Smiley Smile*, *Wild Honey*, *Friends*—were countercultural or retro, they weren't part of a mind-blowing spiritual advance. They didn't fit into the sensitive masterpiece, *Pet Sounds*-centric perspective of *Crawdaddy*, the first magazine devoted to serious writing about rock music, begun in 1966. Nor did they fit the Beatles-centric critiques in *Rolling Stone* from San Francisco, started up in 1967. These perspectives, including Siegel's, assumed an idea of rock music progression that failed to explain the peculiar story line being traced by the Beach Boys. Unless their music didn't have any story line at all.

For loyal fans, it could feel like the best of times. The group was releasing a lot of good music, and you felt as if all of it, their entire career, should be fitting in somewhere with mainstream rock assumptions and attitudes. But for the most part, their music did not, and this led to a strange feeling of weightlessness if you were a fan. The Beach Boys weren't avant-garde loft jazz or experimental, atonal classical music or Bulgarian folk music that assumed a small, special audience. They were a pop group, with a lot of big hits, who once had a big audience. Yet judged by prevailing rock music standards, they didn't exist.

Undergirding much of the writing, in the publicity and reviews in those days about the Beatles and Dylan, or Siegel's on the Beach Boys, were two late '60s ideas about how rock as art differed from pop music as entertainment. Brian being described as the surfer who discovered God connected with countercultural beliefs about the access to wisdom available to rock stars as sensitized artists resembling the Romantic poets, so sensitized they might run off the rails of regular life like Lord Byron, Van Gogh, and Jack Kerouac. The Beatles or Bob Dylan as artists progressing from album to album connected with mainstream ideas about serious painters or musicians or authors having stages and periods, like Picasso, Miles Davis, and Ernest Hemingway. You could check out such changes just by looking at the Beatles' and Dylan's album covers in the '60s. Progress in rock music was proof of the progress of the counterculture, affirmation that the optimism of the early '60s had been relocated, not lost.

After *Smile* was shelved, these generalizations couldn't explain the Beach Boys' career. And if that couldn't be explained by the prevailing ideas about rock-as-art progress, maybe there wasn't anything left to explain. Maybe the Beach Boys had excelled at entertainment, almost elevated themselves into art with *Pet Sounds*, and collapsed back into mere entertainment. That was the assumption behind those *Dance, Dance, Dance* liner notes. It explained why the four albums on Capitol after *Pet Sounds* had so little impact.

Unless you gave those albums a close listen. And then they didn't sound like random filler mixed with potential hits, mere entertainment. They sounded like self-aware, rock-as-art-form creations. *Smiley Smile* was a stoned commentary on the fact that *Smile* didn't exist. *Wild Honey* was an intentional DIY, back to basics, a statement from the home studio that anticipated Dylan's soon-to-follow *John Wesley Harding*. *Friends* was *Pet Sounds* mellowing out while moving to Laurel Canyon. That's how fans heard those new albums, and why we felt they fit into the whole of the Beach Boys' entire career. It was also one reason the albums received thoughtful reviews from rock critics like Robert Christgau and Richard Goldstein. They were reviewable; they invited you to think about them.

This was more than a pop music puzzle. Inside much Beach Boys melancholy lies an anxiety about dislocation, about not fitting in, about feeling that, as one famous track on *Pet Sounds* was titled, "I Just Wasn't Made for These Times." Some, often including Mike Love, heard that anxiety as being at odds with the songs about having teenage fun as one of the gang. Others of us heard both the anxiety and the fun as intertwined expressions of adolescence and coming-of-age in the postwar suburbs, elevated beyond those specifics on *Pet Sounds*, and revisited throughout Brian Wilson's career.

When the Beach Boys first fell out of favor and then into their pit of incomprehensibility, that doubled the reality of not being made for these times, for both the band and their fans. If you really felt the Beach Boys were making pop music that spoke to you—and we did—you felt compelled to find the story, or theory, or generalization that either created or revealed the connection between pop band and pop audience. That connection had disappeared on the *Dance, Dance, Dance* liner notes, but its slow excavation was beginning as the '70s began.

In September 1971, a full-page ad ran in the *Village Voice* and much of the alternative press with this headline: "For a Dollar and an Old *Surfin' Safari* LP, We'll Send You a Dry New Reprise LP by (Believe It) 1971's Beach Boys—*Surf's Up*." A month later, *Rolling Stone* put the Beach Boys on the cover and published the first of a two-part extended profile by Tom Nolan, "The Beach Boys: A California Saga."[1]

The group was at the cusp of its comeback, soon to play Carnegie Hall and appear on the soundtrack of *Five Summer Stories*. Reprise was rolling out the publicity, emphasizing the contrast in the band's career, but unlike Siegel in 1967, hyping the Beach Boys now as just up-to-date, not cutting-edge hip. Most noteworthy, Nolan's long article ("with additional material by David Felton") found a way to place Brian and the Beach Boys into a career-spanning context, covering Wilson family life before they were famous; touring when they were rich, young, and horny; and their current contributions and estrangements inside the band. The article deployed a psychological frame that was an adjustment to the earlier ideas about tortured, sensitive artists, and ditched the expectation of progress, to find the longer connections: the conflicts with Murry, the dynamics between three brothers and a cousin, and the contrast between the early suburban life and the life of pop stardom.

By 1971, reporting from inside the flowering of pop hippiedom was no longer the story. After Charles Manson, Altamont, and the never-ending, ever-evolving Vietnam War, the continuing existence of the battered but functioning Beach Boys was the story. Nolan's journalism assumed a connection between that career-length saga and the shared individual experiences of the *Rolling Stone* readership, rather than offering just an insider peek into the lives of the rock rich and famous. The music was deemphasized in its specifics, more important as a signifier of shared culture than a source of groundbreaking revelation.

This matched the larger psychological turn in baby boomer pop music. The biggest album of the early '70s was Carole King's *Tapestry*, comfortably wrapping some of her early pop hits as a Brill Building girl group composer into the introspective, singer-songwriter, domestic groove of her new songs and public persona. This success fulfilled a desire to hear an intact individual psyche that had passed through both early '60s idealism and late '60s counterculture, as well as some of the changes in gender role expectations. It wasn't an accident that the voice writing and singing was female.

Carole King hit the cultural bull's-eye, but this new demand for a vulnerable presentation of self could create traumas for less savvy and grounded public figures. One recurring theme in Nolan's piece was the difficulty in knowing when Brian was being honest and when he was "putting you on." I interpret this as one put-upon pop star's accommodation to the culture's desire and the recording industry's need for personal revelation as part of the new promotional package. Brian used a shifty false self for protection. By 1971, he had the put-on in place and is still using it today. You want an interview, you got it. Want some personal exposure, here's a little. Gotta go now, have a nice day.

The second installment of Nolan's Beach Boys saga appeared

Tom Smucker

in the November 11, 1971, issue of *Rolling Stone*. It followed directly behind the enormously long first installment of "Fear and Loathing in Las Vegas" by Raoul Duke, aka Hunter S. Thompson, a journalist participating and reporting from inside a scene, who was moving to a scene inside his own drug-addled head. I see symmetry in a journalist pulling back inside himself and the journalist Tom Nolan pulling himself out of the picture and letting the Beach Boys and their father and their manager speak for themselves. Soon, Beach Boys fans as well would be speaking up for themselves, and would begin shaping a new public story about the group, eventually reshaping not just the history but actual events.

I suppose I was using a related approach for my own two-part "Beach Boys—A Fan Tells All" in the July and August 1972 issue of *Creem*. As the title makes obvious, in the article I presented myself as a fan, but one fortified by ideas about pop music from meeting and reading Robert Christgau, Ellen Willis, Richard Goldstein, and Greil Marcus in the late '60s; this legitimized the fan's perspective as an important component of pop music's context. Editor Dave Marsh and the *Creem* vibe allowed me to lay out why and how I loved the group, missteps included.

In preparation, I attended a lot of concerts, sometimes stood backstage, never interviewed anyone, never intruded, and landed on a sweet spot. The Beach Boys had released *Surf's Up*, were eager for coverage in *Creem*, were getting the push in publicity and advertising from Reprise, and had not yet released *Carl and the Passions: So Tough*, which I would find boring, a first-ever reaction for me to a Beach Boys LP. My front-cover memoir in *Creem* might be, I believe, the first long defense in print of every Beach

Boys recording from *Surfin' Safari* to *Surf's Up*, and proof that it was possible to listen to all of their music as an unbroken whole.

The article generated so much mail from hard-core Beach Boys devotees that I tried to start a fanzine, but failed. Shortly thereafter, the real fan clubs and newsletters began popping up, frequently, but not exclusively around Los Angeles. I like to imagine that my success in placing the Beach Boys on the front cover of *Creem* helped push this fannish activity into existence, that it was a "Hey, I'm not alone" moment. Whatever the reality, the club and those newsletters became incubators for people who helped shape a new, useful way of thinking about the Beach Boys and Brian Wilson, and then helped recover some big chunks of Brian's music.

Domenic Priore has an excellent summary of this influential fan-based subculture's creation in the chapter "An Underground Train" of his *Smile: The Story of Brian Wilson's Lost Masterpiece.*[2] These were not music biz insiders, PR professionals, or hustlers, but devotee-advocates. Included in Priore's history are Alice Lillie, the founder of Beach Boys Freaks United, a real fan's fan club and an important hub for finding interconnections; Priore himself; musicians Nick Walusco and Darian Sahanaja, who would eventually form the heart of Brian Wilson's touring band and help Brian complete, perform, and record *Smile*; and author David Leaf, publisher of the Brian-focused newsletter *Pet Sounds*.

There's a book and documentary in all this, about fans creating a new infrastructure that forces the resurrection and redirection of a major pop music act. David Leaf would parlay his *Pet Sounds* newsletter into 1978's *The Beach Boys and the California Myth*, the first full-length interpretation of the entire career of the Beach

Boys and Brian Wilson. Published as an oversized paperback with lots of pictures—a pop music coffee table book, so to speak—it included biographical detail and briefly quoted from the earlier Siegel and Dalton journalism, but put everything in the context of the music. I buy into Leaf's Brian-thwarted-by-the-band thesis, although I'm not a behind-the-scenes guy and I'm more shaped by and identify with whatever recordings and live concerts are available to me, and lots of those did not include Brian physically. But that's not the point. Leaf showed it was possible to have a workable theory about the Beach Boys and all of their music that produced a book-length narrative, as if they were Bob Dylan, or Miles Davis, or the Beatles, or Picasso. The era of the befuddled author assigned Beach Boys liner notes was over. The Beach Boys, it was now obvious, were possible to put into words.

Leaf would continue to shape a public perception of Brian and the group. He wrote the excellent liner notes for the great 1990 two-CD reissues, wrote the liner notes for the 1993 boxed set *Good Vibrations: Thirty Years of the Beach Boys*, and helped expand that compilation so it included at least eight previously unreleased *Smile* session tracks on the second CD. Leaf also contributed to 1995's Don Was documentary and CD, *Brian Wilson: "I Just Wasn't Made for These Times."* In 2001, Leaf organized and produced the cable TV special and eventual DVD *An All-Star Tribute to Brian Wilson* at Radio City featuring Elton John, Paul Simon, Billy Joel, David Crosby, Carly Simon, and then Brian himself singing "Heroes and Villains" for the first time in public in over three decades. The production was not, noticeably, a tribute to the Beach Boys. Leaf was a part of what I called Brian Wilson's brain trust in my rave review of *Smile*, and I meant it as a compliment.

....

"*DEATH OF A BEACH BOY*: Drummer Dennis Wilson Drowns" shouted the half-page headline on the front of the *New York Post*, December 29, 1983. A tragic end to a complicated rock-and-roll life, a tabloid bonanza, and a way to frame a book-length biography of the group. In 1979, Dave Marsh's *Born to Run: The Bruce Springsteen Story*, an enthusiastic, fast-paced biography of New Jersey's rock-and-roll savior, became the surprise first book-length rock biography best seller. Since there were already a number of Beatles bios, the Beach Boys seemed like an obvious next choice. Centering the story of the group on Dennis, to put it simply and cynically, insured a beginning, a middle, and an end. As the details of the last years of his life emerged, it was clear that, as one of his ex-wives described it, by the time he dove into the water at Marina del Ray, he was already dead. There would be no new revelations about his demise that might complicate the ending.

I don't much care for the book this tragedy produced, 1986's *Heroes and Villains: The True Story of the Beach Boys* by Stephen Gaines. There's too much emphasis on the scandalous details, too much sex and drugs and not enough rock and roll. How did all this relate to the music? But to be honest, I do remember feeling vindicated at the time in my fandom by the fact that a full-length biography of the Beach Boys had been published, even though I was upset that it took the sad life of Dennis Wilson to give the book a focus.

Rereading it now, I'm wondering why interviewees were willing to reveal so many intimate details, and why the book believes those details reveal the "true story." Then I remember the 1987 presidential campaign of Senator Gary Hart. He and we thought that Hart might become the new JFK and the media wouldn't interfere with his personal life, respecting a boundary still in place in the early '60s. But Hart was exposed, some might say double-crossed, for lying about fooling around while his wife was back home in Colorado; the media descended on him, ending his campaign, and we got stuck with George Bush the First.[3] By the mid-'80s, the psychological turn that began in the early '70s was obliterating the distinction between public and private, in politics and pop culture. All the more reason for public figures to learn how to use vulnerability as a mask, or to present a reassuringly tough veneer.

The success of Gaines's book led to the first of the TV movies about the Beach Boys, 1989's *Summer Dreams*. Centered on Dennis and otherwise spotty, portraying Brian as a dim-witted wimp, it's worth at least one viewing to enjoy the cheap hippie wigs and paste-on beards the cast all start wearing after Brian smokes pot and takes LSD in the '60s. All such movies must end on a high note, and this one concludes after Dennis's death with the triumphant 1984 concert on the Fourth of July at the Washington Mall, the same high note used to conclude 1985's documentary *The Beach Boys: An American Band*. Wigs and misrepresentations included, both movies underlined what the book had already proved: it was possible to tell a story about the Beach Boys that encompassed the length of their career, some of their music, and, more or less, everyone in the band.

I didn't buy or read 1991's *Wouldn't It Be Nice: My Own Story*, supposedly written by Brian Wilson with Todd Gold, but actually controlled by the discredited Dr. Landy. A quick peek inside made it obvious to me that the book wasn't even ghostwritten in Brian's voice. As an example of a form of hustling and psychiatric malpractice peculiar to the Hollywood side of LA—the shrink who felt entitled to ghostwrite his famous patient's autobiography—it's also proof of that story's value. In the twenty years since those *Dance, Dance, Dance* liner notes, it had become easy to put the Beach Boys into words, and now it mattered who got to pick those words.

The only book or movie mentioned in this chapter that wasn't absorbed into public consciousness about the Beach Boys, *My Own Story* was part of a fabrication so inaccurate and malicious that it almost erased the real Brian Wilson and the real Beach Boys from public consciousness. When I noticed I wasn't interested in reading the book, I was also noticing that I was losing interest in Brian Wilson and the Beach Boys altogether. Luckily, *My Own Story* was published as Landy was being pried loose from Brian, who hadn't produced any interesting music since his first solo album in 1988. That would change.

Timothy White's 418-page *The Nearest Faraway Place: Brian Wilson, the Beach Boys, and the Southern California Experience*, published in paperback in 1996,[4] ends with the wedding of Brian and Melinda on February 6, 1995. White does a thorough, maybe too thorough job of setting the backstory of the Wilson family in Kansas and earlier generations from Ohio, New York, and Sweden; the construction of twentieth-century Southern California; and the creation of the LA studios and record companies. Most important, White liked the Beach Boys as people and loved their music. There's a deadline dash toward the end of the updated paperback edition, rushing the story past Landy's removal and on to the wedding of Brian and Melinda—an actual high note, a good place to end, the beginning of Brian's real comeback. The book itself was part of that comeback's intellectual underpinnings, proof that the world of publishing and the book-buying public were ready to support an honest and affectionate biography of the Beach Boys without tying it together with false optimism or getting lost in the scandalous details.

That meant there was now a commonly shared story out there about the Beach Boys and Brian Wilson, whether it was a few random details vaguely remembered by largely uninterested civilians or the encyclopedia of details held by the army of hardcore devotees. A shared story, however, did not bring an end to the competition inside the group over biographical emphasis.

Full House heartthrob John Stamos, Mike Love's buddy and the occasional drummer in Mike's Beach Boys band, remade the earlier Beach Boys TV movie in 2000 as *The Beach Boys: An American Family*. Twice as long, with much improved hippie-era hair, deemphasizing Dennis and focusing on Mike, the movie repeated the ridiculously wimpish portrayal of Brian, contrasting him with Mike and the sensible realists at Capitol Records, and representing Van Dyke Parks and the entire late '60s LA hip, pop culture milieu as a B-movie drug-addled, lava-lamp slumber party. This perspective influenced by Mike Love undercut its own credibility with a melodramatic portrayal of rivals, but it worked well as an organizing principal for some Beach Boys' career-spanning compilations.

Sounds of Summer, 2003's thirty-track CD on Capitol, would sell 3 million copies and then generate a 2004 edition with a DVD and a 2005 *Platinum Edition* with sixty tracks over three

CDs. Less interested in history than the *Good Vibrations* boxed set, sequenced for flow, more like a concert, most likely by Mike, *Sounds of Summer* steered clear of interesting obscurities and stuck to big hits or could-have-been hits tilted toward some of Mike's lesser achievements. Unlike the earliest Capitol reissues, which sounded random ("Frosty the Snowman"?), the *Sounds of Summer* trilogy followed *Endless Summer*'s example—proof that there was more than one way to make sense of the Beach Boys.

The dramatic resurgence of a Brian-focused history came with the completion and performance of *Smile* in 2004. Lengthy raves included Bernard Weinraub in the *New York Times*, Bob Chaundry for *BBC News*, Richard Harrington in the *Washington Post*, Robert Christgau in *Rolling Stone*, Issac Guzman in the *New York Daily News*, myself in the *Village Voice*, Malcolm Jones in *Newsweek*, John Payne in LA *Weekly*, Ted Gioia in the *Threepenny Review*, Scott Staton in the *New York Review of Books*, Brian Levine in *Scientific American Mind*, Douglas Wolk in the *Nation*, Lucy Dallas in the *Times Literary Supplement*, Michael Anton in the *Claremont Review*, and Paul Cooper in *Worker's Liberty*.

The breadth of the acclaim was startling. I only found one single paragraph of dissent. More startling was the across-the-board understanding of Brian Wilson, his relationship to the Beach Boys, the history of *Smile*, and the group's place in pop music. The raves were all built on shared assumptions about the Beach Boys and Brian Wilson's significance, whatever the reviewer's politics or position in pop or high culture.

Peter Ames Carlin's 2006 *Catch a Wave: The Rise, Fall and Redemption of the Beach Boys' Brian Wilson* solidified this consensus, updating the history of the group through Brian's comeback and the completion and performance of *Smile*. The title itself showed the shift from a story of the group as a whole to a story centering on Brian. David Leaf's paradigm, first published as a book in 1978, had become the standard for thinking about the group as a whole almost thirty years later.

Love and Mercy, the 2014 movie, built on these same shared assumptions and, whether accurate or not in every detail, stood out as a really good movie. As a fan, I was pleased to see that we were past the era of bad hippie wigs, of Charles Manson, of Brian's first joint, of the piano in the sandbox, of the triumphant big concert happy ending. This movie finally showed the recording studio as an actual place where people worked and made music, and portrayed Brian Wilson as an actual person. Each time I've seen the movie—and I've watched it a lot—I come away feeling like, okay, we got there: an honest representation of what the Beach Boys and Brian Wilson created, and some of what made it so easy and some of what made it so hard.

Focusing much less on Brian and more on himself, Mike's 2016 memoir *Good Vibrations: My Life as a Beach Boy* is a worthwhile read. Mike can be perceptive writing about himself and his past when he's staying clear of temptations to badmouth his rivals. Brian's 2016 memoir *I Am Brian Wilson* is less orderly, more like Bob Dylan's 2004 *Chronicles: Volume One*, and important as the permanent historical rebuke and replacement of Landy's literary fraud.

In the fifty or so years since their late '60s fall off the pop music pedestal, the Beach Boys have traveled from being a group it was hard, if not impossible, to tell a story about to being a group whose story gets told and retold. Some of that's just the passage of time, but most of it's the result of all the creative music they've made available live and on record over the years, as well as a lot of advocacy and explanation by biographers, journalists, managers, publicists, anthologists, curators, and fans. The Beach Boys were never America's Band—that's reaching too far. But their struggle to have a story and make a space for their story is itself one of those great American stories, and that's good enough.

20

Summer's Gone, the Endless Summer

....

There's a ghoulish music biz jest that claims the best career move Elvis (or Jim Morrison or Michael Jackson) ever made was dying, capping off careers once they were past their prime. Brian Wilson proved the opposite. The best career move he ever made was staying alive, defying expectations, returning to recording and performing, capping off a career with a surprising late-life comeback.

This personal drama of collapse and revival echoed all the cycles in the popularity of his music. The early 1960s hits went out of fashion in the late '60s and roared back in the mid-'70s. *Pet Sounds* got double-crossed by the record label on release, and was crowned years later by the same label with boxed set and reissue accolades. *Smile* became famous because it did not exist, and then unbelievably, became famous again because it did. Brian was famous for his fear of live performance, and then began a late-life endless tour.

Alongside this bumpy group history ran a parallel history of the recorded pop music art form. And alongside those ran the larger history of a generation trying to come to terms with changing ideas about race and gender and America's place in the world, from the postwar confidence and affluence of the '50s and early '60s through the economic, social, and political ups and downs of the following five decades.

Over the years, there have been attempts by the group to sing about their own history as a group, but that's an unruly story to sum up in a song. More successful have been Brian's songs that focus on himself, which we can take as representing the larger group as well. Some recent recordings, rarely if ever performed in concert, are elegiac farewells: "Think About the Days," "From There to Back Again," "Pacific Coast Highway," "Summer's Gone," "This Beautiful Day," "The Last Song." In their own way, they're remarkable, partly as personal reflections, and partly as proof that Brian and the Beach Boys have created a public story that stretches beyond five decades. It's a long way from "Keep an Eye on Summer" to "Summer's Gone," with a lot of music in between. And who knows, there may be new surprises. But reaching a stage where you can reference your own history while keeping the music from that history fresh is a real pop music achievement.

How all this music will be heard, if at all, in the future depends on how the world the Beach Boys have inhabited is understood in the future. At the moment, that world is fading as the origin of a shared way of life, while growing in stature as one important origin of how we make popular art. Southern California is as likely to be associated with *Straight Outta Compton* as with *Surfin' USA* these days. That's an improvement, and in the long run, a connection. It makes the Beach Boys one part of a larger story, not the whole of it, which was and would be a lie. Los Angeles is an established big city now, not the progenitor of an emerging way of life. We gaze in fear and awe more toward the northwest, from Silicon Valley to Seattle, toward Microsoft, Google, Apple, Amazon, Tesla. For music, we listen to Nashville and Atlanta. But some of the template we use to do that can be traced back to Hawthorne, California.

With *Smile* completed, we can dream along with *Glimpses'* time-traveling stereo repairman about what album could come next. As I write, I'd like to imagine forty-seven minutes of interlocking white American pop music addressing the spread of the institution of black chattel slavery somewhere in the mix. I know that's not likely, but neither was the reemergence of *Smile*. And in the end, Beach Boys music moves toward hope.

EPILOGUE

Suggestions

....

A chronological discography follows the bibliography. Not a guide for audiophiles, these are some suggestions about products related to the Beach Boys available in the physical universe and the digital cloud, including recordings from Beach Boys' friends, ex-wives, and admirers.

I've left off information that would go into a collector's guide, for those looking for original pressings, and so on. There are other books for that. This is an overview of music that has been rereleased, anthologized, reformatted, and rearranged with different content in different countries, available as often used as new. Enjoy.

Vinyl

The best part of twelve-inch albums is the front cover. The very first album, *Surfin' Safari*, has the original promo shot at Paradise Cove with the woody, and *Surfer Girl* has the other original promo shot with the Boys in their Pendletons carrying a surfboard. Dare we say iconic? It's the image refashioned on the historical monument to the Beach Boys in their hometown,

Hawthorne. But of those early albums, I rate *Little Deuce Coupe* at the top. There are no Beach Boys on the cover, just the custom hot rod (the Boys appear on the back). Nonetheless, it's all good stuff in the grooves, including "Be True to Your School." *Shut Down Volume 2* has a great shot on the front of the Boys standing around Dennis's muscle car, and that wonderfully mysterious title, but two weak tracks. *Shut Down Volume 1* is indeed a lame rip-off, only of historical value as proof of Capitol's early disregard for Beach Boys music.

From their next vinyl era, I recommend *Smiley Smile*. It's got a real hippie cover, front and back, with a great quote ascribed to "Indian Wisdom." What could be groovier than that? It's also one of my favorite albums and hard to find in vinyl. Next, I'd recommend *Sunflower*, another poor-selling (rich) hippie album, but only if you get a version that includes the shot of Mike Love in his guru robes, preferably inside the gatefold. As a companion, I recommend the *Spring* album by Brian's wife Marilyn and sister-in-law Diane, in vinyl with the arty double fold with the life masks on the cover and fuzzy-toned photo portrait inside. *Spring* is hard to locate on vinyl and rarely available streaming, but is available on CD without the cool graphics.

Of the big early '70s comeback records, my favorite in vinyl is *Surf's Up*. As much as anything, this album's cover announced that the Beach Boys were making a return to the big time. And then, of course, there's the vinyl *Endless Summer* cover, with the old hippie Beach Boys hiding in the foliage to observe the return of their old surf, car, and summer songs. And look for *The Beach Boys Love You*. This strange but compelling record works well in vinyl—you can take it just one side at a time—and Dean Torrence of Jan and

Dean designed the cover. Reprise released lots of copies, and then the Beach Boys left the label, so there are more than the average number of factory-sealed mint-condition originals out there.

I can't in good conscience recommend the Brother/Reprise twofers of the orphaned 1967–1968 albums because the covers are so stupid. But the recordings themselves were high quality.

Vinyl jazz buffs: flute and sax virtuoso Charles Lloyd had connections to Mike Love through Transcendental Meditation, and in the early '70s recorded two mellow fusion albums with contributions from Mike and the other Beach Boys, *Waves* and *Warm Waters*. Both are cheaper on the internet, in the original vinyl versions, than on CD. Buy them and dazzle your friends with proof that Mike Love collaborated with the same guy (Lloyd) who collaborated with Billy Higgins and Geri Allen. Also check out, via the internet, Lloyd's beautifully recorded video of his eight-minute-plus improvisation on "Caroline No."

CDs

Reissues and anthologies are floating through Amazon, eBay, and elsewhere, sometimes in multiple versions differing in content but sharing the same cover graphics. I highly recommend the four-CD boxed set, or whatever it is called now, *Good Vibrations: Thirty Years of the Beach Boys*, with the great liner notes by David Leaf. Likewise, the twofers of their old albums on CD, with notes by Leaf. These were originally released in 1990, and then remastered and rereleased in 2001. The newer ones do indeed sound better. The 2001 versions have small shots of both vinyl album front covers on the back of the CD. If you're going to buy just one Beach Boys CD, pick one of these. And watch out: Capitol has recently re-rereleased single CDs of single albums that had been on the twofers.

Here are nine non–Beach Boys CDs related to this book, in no particular order, that I find interesting. They're less likely to be available on a streaming service than what I've listed in the discography. Included is a sentence about why I like them; deleted is most of the information other than the label. Maybe you can find them online or in a Salvation Army Store used CD bin.

Girl Group Greats. Rhino. Twenty great examples of where the Beach Boys and the Beatles have their roots. Starts with "Heat Wave" and ends with "Party Lights." There are other girl group CD anthologies out there that are not as good, so look for this one from Rhino.

Stick Shift. The Duals. Collectable Records. The African American duo's hot rod guitar hit, for the historical record. Did they pick their name because there were two of them, or . . . ?

Long Promised Road: Songs of Dennis and Carl Wilson. Adam Marsland's Chaos Band featuring Evie Sands and Alan Boyd. Karma Frog. Delivers what it promises. Evie Sands singing "Trader," wow. A recorded live tribute to the Two Other Brothers.

Spring. Produced by Brian Wilson. Rhino. This anthology includes some singles and is hard to find on the streaming services; worth purchasing on CD if you can't find the vinyl, along with *The Honeys* anthology on Capitol. Brian's first wife Marilyn, her sister Dianne, and their cousin

Ginger were the Honeys. Minus Ginger, the sisters were Spring.

The Four Freshmen Live at Butler University. Creative World. Brian's modern jazz vocal idols cover "Surfer Girl' while they're still the top dogs of collegiate concerts. Times were changing.

Cassettes

Maybe these four cassettes exist in some other format, but I've never seen them.

Kokomo, Tutti Frutti. Elektra. The Beach Boys and Little Richard on a cassette single with a picture of Tom Cruise on the front. It's real, I own it.

Happy Endings. The Beach Boys and Little Richard. *California Girls*. The Beach Boys. Critique-ATCO. Cassette single from the motion picture *The Telephone*. It's real, I own it.

A Vision Shared: A Tribute to Woody Guthrie and Leadbelly. Folkways. Bob Dylan covers "Pretty Boy Floyd." U2 covers "Jesus Christ." Brian Wilson covers "Goodnight Irene."

Rock 'n' Roll City. Radio Shack. Mike Love and Dean Torrence. Mike rocks out on "The Letter" and "The Locomotion."

Digital

Lots of old Beach Boys concert recordings are getting released digitally for downloading or streaming to protect copyrights on previously unreleased tapes before they hit fifty years. All of them are fun, and few, so far, contain surprises. After a while, the novelty wears off when listening to the screaming young girls who wish they were at a Beatles concert. *Keep an Eye on Summer: The Beach Boys Sessions 1964*, released digitally in December 2014, is a wonderful collection of studio sessions from the *Shut Down Volume 2*, *All Summer Long* era. A pre–*Pet Sounds* peek at the Beach Boys and the Wrecking Crew at work in the studio, and a snapshot of Carl's contributions on guitar. Surprising how hard the instrumentals minus the vocals can rock. Worth a listen.

If you like *Smiley Smile*, don't miss downloading or streaming *Portland Smiles* (unavailable in physical format) from Tender Loving Empire. It's a perfect tribute-cover from an assortment of northwest indies.

If you have fifteen hours to kill and want to give Mike Love a chance, try the audiobook of *Good Vibrations: My Life as a Beach Boy* read by Mike Love himself. Don't focus on every detail, especially about the lawsuits, and just take it as an interesting guy in the seat next to yours telling you his life story during a transcontinental bus ride. You'll find yourself drawn in as Mike embellishes his reading with a little singing, some chuckling, and some choking up. He's in his mid-seventies now, and his speaking voice sounds a lot like the current Clint Eastwood's, but nicer.

Books

The biographies by David Leaf, Timothy White, and Peter Ames Carlin are all worth reading. Other trustworthy authors on the

Beach Boys beat include Keith Badman, Domenic Priore, Jon Stebbins, and John Tobler. Stephen J. McParland has compiled his own library of books about the Beach Boys, surf music, beach party movies, hot rods, and celebrities, including from his home base in Australia.

If you want one little book to help keep track of all the music, I recommend *Brian Wilson and the Beach Boys: The Complete Guide to Their Music* by Andrew Doe and John Tobler (Omnibus Press, 2004). It's only 176 pages with short, to-the-point paragraphs about every song on every album. Small, clearly written and laid out, mass-market paperback size, it fits comfortably on my bookshelf between *Gidget* and *Any Old Way You Choose It*.

ACKNOWLEDGMENTS

....

In 1967, I was lucky enough to be living down the block from one of the locations where rock criticism was being invented, and although I knew enough to know I could never turn it into a livelihood, it changed if not saved my life. Like so many others, that intellectual framework helped me become me. Gratitude to Richard Goldstein, Greil Marcus, Ellen Willis; and especially to Robert Christgau, mentor, rabbi, original thinker, advisor, and best of all, friend and neighbor for so many years, through the good times and the tears. On our sixth decade now. A college dropout, I learned to write as an occasional contributor to the *Village Voice*, in its prime a place where the editors were both smart and generous, and I got the best. Christgau, of course, and Goldstein, and Karin Durbin and Chuck Eddy and Thulani Davis. Thanks to Eric Weisbard and Ann Powers for including me in the EMP/MoPOP gathering, a place to listen and be heard, and to Evelyn McDonnell, for thinking of me for this series—all three part of the *Voice* diaspora. Thanks to Stephen P. Hull for taking a chance on this old Beach Boys fan with no proof that he could write a book. And special thanks to all in New Hampshire and Texas for making the transfer so smooth.

Middle Church proved that great gospel music could come out of a tolerant, inclusive Christianity, and it opened me to think more about those connections. I hear music in the air. Thanks to the entire past and present congregation, the deacons and elders, choirs, Gordon, Jacqui, and especially, in loving memory, Jerriesse. CWA Local 1101 gave me a life with an income, a pension, and benefits. The people who brought you the weekend. Summertime mountain friends tolerated me as a reclusive guest hiding out with his laptop: Dana and Paul, Georgia and Steven, Bonnie and Mel, Amy and Bill, Claude and Amy. Thanks to Pat and everyone for keeping the RMC afloat. Thanks to Frank for memories of El Monte, Asuza, and Vietnam. Thanks to Yvonne for making the Midwest migration and LA in the '50s and '60s real for me, and for marrying my twin. Thanks to Dr. Clements, Dr. Slovin, and Dr. McBride for keeping me alive.

Most of all, to Sarah and Aaron, for everything, especially for proving that children whose dad listens too often to *Pet Sounds Sessions* can still grow up into wonderful adults with their own preferences in music. Don't believe the hype. And to Sarah and Bill, for bringing Lillian into the world to remind us that life can be a wonderful discovery and music is always mysterious and special. Ba-ba-ba-Ba-Barbara Ann.

And for Laura. It's more than fifty years since our first night together on 110th Street. In the morning I looked through your record collection —Dylan, Baez, Brahms, and Otis Redding—and decided I was in trouble. So I gave you my second copy of 20/20 and confessed that I played a lot of Beach Boys and you should give the LP a listen and see if you could stand them. You did, you said it was okay, and we're still together. But the best part is that you don't even remember this! You still believe in me and I still believe in you. Forever.

NOTES

....

1. Harmony and Discord

1. Bob Hyde, "Track by Track Annotation" booklet, in *The Doo-wop Box* (Los Angeles: Rhino Records).

2. Mike Love with James S. Hirsch, *Good Vibrations: My Life as a Beach Boy* (New York: Blue Rider Press, 2016), 28.

3. Dean Torrence, *Surf City: The Jan and Dean Story* (New York: Select Books, 2016), 41.

4. An unfortunate apostrophe survives from the original album. Surfers Rule because they are royalty, not because surfers follow a rulebook.

5. Harvey Cox, *Fire from Heaven* (New York: Addison-Wesley, 1995), 60–65. Peter Guralnick, *Last Train to Memphis: The Rise of Elvis Presley* (Boston: Little, Brown, 1994), 75. Cheryl J. Sanders, *Saints in Exile* (New York: Oxford University Press, 1996). Ann Taves, "Shouting Methodists," in *Fits, Trances, and Visions: Experiencing Religion and Explaining Experience from Wesley to James* (Princeton: Princeton University Press, 1999), 76–117.

6. Bicoastal snob alert: Columbus, Indiana, is ranked as the sixth-best American city for architecture by the American Institute of Architects (AIA), and contains seven National Historic Landmarks among its numerous examples of modernist public schools, libraries, and churches.

7. Ross Barbour, *Now You Know: The Story of the Four Freshmen*

(Lake Geneva, WI, 1998), 64. An original Freshman, Ross Barbour credits three acts with inventing the pop college concert rather than college dance: Louis Armstrong, Dave Brubeck, and the Freshmen. I would add the Kingston Trio.

8. Phillip Lambert, *Inside the Music of Brian Wilson* (New York: Continuum, 2007), 130.

9. Peter Carlin, *Catch a Wave: The Rise, Fall and Redemption of the Beach Boys' Brian Wilson* (New York: Rodale, 2006), 18. Love, *Good Vibrations*, 28. Timothy White, *The Nearest Faraway Place: Brian Wilson, the Beach Boys, and the Southern California Experience* (New York: Henry Holt, Owl Books, 1996), 79.

10. Barbour, *Now You Know*, 17.

11. I don't count "He Came Down" because it's a Transcendental Meditation/Christian mash-up, or Brian's solo Christmas CD from 2005. I leave out Dennis Wilson's Jesus references on *Pacific Ocean Blue* because that's very much a solo album. Malotte, by the way, was based in LA, and composed soundtracks for Disney animations, most famously for *Ferdinand the Bull*.

12. Brian Wilson, *I Am Brian Wilson* (Boston: Da Capo, 2016), 170.

2. Cars and Guitars

1. Stephen B. Goddard, *Getting There: The Epic Struggle between Road and Rail In The American Century* (Chicago: University of Chicago Press, 1994), 185–86. Steven Parissien, *The Life of the Automobile* (New York: St. Martin's, 2013), 186–87.

2. Rob Burt, *Surf City, Drag City* (New York: Blandford, 1986), 25. Stephen J. McParland, *Surf Beat: The Dick Dale Story* (North Strathfield, AU: C Music, 2000), 11, 12. Alan Di Perna and Brad Tolinksy, *Play It Loud* (New York: Doubleday, 2016), 95–99.

3. The popularity of surfing required the reduction in weight of the

original hundred-pound redwood plank surfboard to a twenty-pound shaped foam, finished board. The new board depended on foam, glue, and finish developed during and after World War II.

4. Nelson George, *Where Did Our Love Go? The Rise and Fall of the Motown Sound* (New York: St. Martin's, 1985), 112.

5. Allen Slutsky, "Dr. Licks," in *Standing in the Shadows of Motown: The Life and Music of Legendary Bassist James Jamerson* (Wynnewood, PA: Dr. Licks Publishing, 1989), as quoted by John Entwhistle of the Who in the accompanying instructional CD.

6. *Shut Down Volume 2* was preceded by the *Shut Down* album, a deservedly obscure compilation from Capitol Records of more-or-less car songs, including two from the Beach Boys.

7. The single was indeed just about two minutes, and inexplicably chops off most of the finale, unlike the original album cut and, of course, any live version ever. Some compilations, remastered or otherwise, use the single version, which robs the song of its achievement. Both versions are floating out there, unidentified, in the new world of streaming.

8. The fourth track is a skit.

3. Suburbs and Surf

1. Earl Swift, *The Big Roads* (New York: Mariner Books, 2011).

2. Ian Rusten and John Stebbins, *The Beach Boys in Concert* (Milwaukee: Backbeat Books, 2013), 20–22.

3. Chris Noel, *Matter of Survival: The "War" Jane Never Saw* (Boston: Branden, 1987).

4. Dana Brown, *The Endless Summer Revisited* (Monterey Media DVD, 2000). Bruce Brown's son Dana, also a surf movie

documentarian (*Step into Liquid*), made this movie about the creation and promotion of his father's movie.

5. Matthew Dallek, *The Right Moment: Ronald Reagan's First Victory and the Decisive Turning Point in American Politics* (New York: Oxford University Press, 2004), 60, 61.

6. Richard Rothstein, *The Color of Law: A Forgotten History of How Our Government Segregated America* (New York: W. W. Norton, 2017). This is the best current summary of how residential segregation was imposed by the federal government into the 1950s.

7. Ibid., 86, 87, 278. Where I lived as a kid is referred to here as the Lombard Co-op.

8. Twyla Tharp, *Push Comes to Shove: An Autobiography* (New York: Linda Grey Bantam, 1992), 177–85.

9. Kathie Meyer, "From Combat to Rock 'n' Roll to Santa: Toys for Tots Poster Has Been Repeat Gig for Marine Corps Artist," *Port Townsend Leader*, December 19, 2007.

10. Meg Jacobs, *Panic at the Pump: The Energy Crisis and the Transformation of American Politics in the 1970s* (New York: Hill and Wang, 2016).

11. X-Men, *Pipeline Remix*, promotional copy not for sale, yellow label (Rated "X" Records). Flip side: *Body Mechanic, Remix*, yellow label.

4. Studio and Stage

1. Kent Crowley, *Long Promised Road: Carl Wilson, Soul of the Beach Boys* (London: Jawbone Press, 2015), 23–26.

2. Keith Badman, *The Beach Boys: The Definitive Diary of America's Greatest Band on Stage and in the Studio* (San Francisco: Backbeat Books, 2004), 14.

3. William Bush, "The Kingston Trio," *Frets*, June 1984.

4. Virgil Moorefield, *The Producer as Composer: Shaping the Sounds of Popular Music* (Cambridge, MA: MIT Press, 2010).

5. Ahmir Thompson, "Questlove," in *Mo' Meta Blues: The World According to Questlove*, by Ahmir "Questlove" Thompson and Ben Greenman (New York: Grand Central, 2013), 41–42.

6. Jann Wenner, "Rock and Roll Music," *Rolling Stone*, December 14, 1967: 16.

7. Paul Williams, *Brian Wilson and the Beach Boys: How Deep Is the Ocean?* (New York: Omnibus, 1997), 37–88.

8. This is the address of Mike Love's childhood home, where Mike and Brian would listen to late-night doo-wop on the radio.

9. Peter Buck, "Peter Buck Interviews Brian Wilson," *Mojo*, June 1998: 78–88. Patti Smith, "The Beach Boys Love You," *Hit Parader*, May 15, 1977.

5. Fathers, Shrinks, and Gurus

1. Keith Badman, *The Beach Boys: The Definitive Diary of America's Greatest Band on Stage and in the Studio* (San Francisco: Backbeat Books, 2004), 329.

2. Richard Sennet with Jonathan Cobb, *The Hidden Injuries of Class* (New York: Knopf, 1973).

6. Girlfriends, Wives, and Mothers

1. Kent Crowley, *Long Promised Road: Carl Wilson, Soul of the Beach Boys* (London: Jawbone Press, 2015), 41–43.

8. Jan and Dean

1. Steven J. McParland, *Jan and Dean in Perspective, 1958–1968: The Grand High Potentates of California Rock* (North Strathfield, AU: C Music, 2004), 19. Mark Thomas Passmore, *Dead Man's Curve and Back: The Jan and Dean Story* (Bloomington, IN: 1st Books Library, 2003), 29, 30.

2. Dean Torrence, *Surf City: The Jan and Dean Story* (New York: Select Books, 2016), 127–31.

3. Ibid., 98.

9. Innocence and the Second-Best Pop Album Ever

1. Charles L. Granata, *Wouldn't It Be Nice: Brian Wilson and the Making of the Beach Boys' Pet Sounds* (Chicago: Chicago Review Press, 2003), 186–94.

2. Memoirs by Questlove of the Roots, Brian Wilson, and George Clinton, the mastermind of P-Funk, all have the same coauthor, Ben Greenman. Coincidence?

3. Dave Marsh and John Swenson, *The Rolling Stone Record Guide* (New York: Random House, 1979), 25.

4. Dave Marsh and John Swenson, *The New Rolling Stone Record Guide* (New York: Random House, 1983), 30.

5. *Rolling Stone* 937 (December 11, 2003): 86.

10. Hip and White

1. Nelson Algren and H. E. F. Donahue, *Conversations with Nelson Algren* (New York: Hill and Wang, 1964), 132.

11. The Best Unreleased Pop Album Ever

1. See my website: www.smileysmile.org.

2. Lewis Shiner, *Glimpses* (New York: St. Martin's Griffin, 2001), 82–142.

3. Tom Smucker, "Wilsonian Democracy," *Village Voice*, September 21, 2004, www.villagevoice.com.

4. Benjamin Madley, *An American Genocide: The United States and the California Indian Catastrophe* (New Haven: Yale University Press, 2017).

5. Michael Anton, "Paradise Lost and Regained," *Claremont Review of Books*, Spring 2012, www.claremontinstitute.org.

6. Disc one of the two-disc DVD set *Brian Wilson Presents Smile*. Disc two is a live performance of *Smile*, but not the debut at the Royal Albert Hall in London.

14. Dennis

1. William McKeen, *Everybody Had an Ocean: Music and Mayhem in 1960s Los Angeles* (Chicago: Chicago Review Press, 2017).

15. Carl

1. Kent Crowley, *Long Promised Road: Carl Wilson, Soul of the Beach Boys* (London: Jawbone Press, 2015).

17. Mike

1. Mike Love with James S. Hirsch, *Good Vibrations: My Life as a Beach Boy* (New York: Blue Rider Press), 2016.

2. Tim Spofford, *Lynch Street: The May 1970 Slayings at Jackson State College* (Kent, OH: Kent State University Press, 1988).

19. Storytellers, Historians, and Fans

1. Tom Nolan, "The Beach Boys: A California Saga," *Rolling Stone* 94, October 28, 1971; *Rolling Stone* 95, November 11, 1971.

2. Domenic Priore, *Smile: The Story of Brian Wilson's Lost Masterpiece* (London: Sanctuary Press, 2005), 146–63.

3. Matt Bai, *All the Truth Is Out: The Week Politics Went Tabloid* (New York: Knopf, 2014).

4. Timothy White, *The Nearest Faraway Place: Brian Wilson, the Beach Boys, and the Southern California Experience* (New York: Henry Holt, Owl Books, 1996).

DISCOGRAPHY

....

To help make sense of over a half century of recorded music, this long but simplified discography is organized chronologically, with relevant music produced by individual Beach Boys, other collaborators, and contemporaries, to give context, inserted into the chronology in the order the music was released in the United States. It doesn't include rereleases or repackaged oldies or albums with Beach Boys guest appearances unless they were important and discussed in this book. It skips singles unless they were unique or historically important, and includes only music that is or was available in some physical manifestation. There are no track lists, contributing musicians' lists, or record numbers, unless those details are related to issues raised in other chapters. No distinctions are made between mono, stereo, duophonic, or quadrophonic. All that would fill a book, and it has: *Surf's Up! The Beach Boys on Record, 1961–1981* by Brad Elliot. Singles and songs appear in quotes, album titles in italics. Some entries have additional comments.

"Surfin'." The Beach Boys. X. November 1961.

Surfin' Safari. The Beach Boys. Capitol. October 1962.

"Sherry." The Four Seasons. Vee-Jay. August 1962.

Surfin' USA. The Beach Boys. Capitol. March 1963. It all comes together here on their second album, the only one to contain real surf music instrumentals.

"Surf City." Jan and Dean. Liberty. May 1963.

Surfer Girl. The Beach Boys. Capitol. September 1963.

Little Deuce Coupe. The Beach Boys. Capitol. October 1963. A powerful mixture of old and new cuts about cars released only a month after their last surf-themed album.

Shut Down, Volume 2. The Beach Boys. Capitol. March 1964. Contains "Fun, Fun, Fun."

"Dead Man's Curve." Jan and Dean. Liberty. May 1964.

All Summer Long. The Beach Boys. Capitol. July 1964.

Beach Boys Christmas Album. The Beach Boys. Capitol. October 1964.

Beach Boys Concert. The Beach Boys. Capitol. October 1964.

The Beach Boys Today! The Beach Boys. Capitol. March 1965.
Prefigures *Pet Sounds* with tracks like "In The Back of My Mind."

Summer Days (And Summer Nights!!). The Beach Boys. Capitol. July 1965. Contains "California Girls."

Beach Boys' Party! The Beach Boys. Capitol. November 1965. Contains "Barbara Ann."

Rubber Soul. The Beatles. Capitol. December 1965.

Pet Sounds. The Beach Boys. Capitol. May 1966.

Best of the Beach Boys. The Beach Boys. Capitol. July 1966.

Revolver. The Beatles. Capitol. August 1966.

"Good Vibrations." The Beach Boys. Capitol. October 1966.

The Temptations Greatest Hits. The Temptations. Motown. November 1966.

Sgt. Pepper's Lonely Hearts Club Band. The Beatles. Capitol. May 1967.

Best of the Beach Boys, Volume 2. The Beach Boys. Capitol. July 1967.

Smiley Smile. The Beach Boys. Capitol. September 1967. A stoner classic that sold poorly but launched a whole new genre.

The Many Moods of Murry Wilson. Murry Wilson. Capitol. October 1967.

Wild Honey. The Beach Boys, Capitol. December 1967. Released three months after *Smiley Smile*, this is another poor-selling, effortless gem.

Song Cycle. Van Dyck Parks. Warner Brothers. December 1967.

Friends. The Beach Boys. Capitol. June 1968.

The Best of the Beach Boys, Volume 3. The Beach Boys. Capitol. August 1968.

Stack o' Tracks. The Beach Boys. Capitol. August 1968.

20/20. The Beach Boys. Capitol. February 1969. This mishmash should not have held together but did.

Sunflower. The Beach Boys. Capitol. August 1970. Another poor-selling album, beautifully produced.

Surf's Up, The Beach Boys. Capitol. August 1971. The group finally recaptures the public's attention.

Carl and the Passions: So Tough (with *Pet Sounds*). The Beach Boys. Capitol. May 1972. An offbeat album that had a following but failed to connect, and suffered by being oddly paired with the reissued *Pet Sounds*.

Spring. Spring. United Artists. July 1972. Beautifully produced, unpretentiously sung by Brian's wife Marilyn and her sister Dianne.

Waves. Charles Lloyd. A & M. October 1972.

Holland. The Beach Boys. Brother-Reprise. January 1973. The second of the ambitious comeback albums to successfully reconnect with the public mood.

The Beach Boys in Concert. The Beach Boys. Brother-Reprise. November 1973.

Endless Summer. The Beach Boys. Capitol. June 1974. And then the first half of their career returned with a vengeance.

Wild Honey and *20/20*. The Beach Boys. Brother-Reprise. July 1974.

Friends and *Smiley Smile*. The Beach Boys. Brother-Reprise. October 1974. Oddly paired. Look for the twofer CD of *Smiley Smile* and *Wild Honey* instead.

Spirit of America. The Beach Boys. Capitol. April 1975.

15 Big Ones. The Beach Boys. Brother-Reprise. July 1976.

Beach Boys '69 (Live in London). The Beach Boys. Capitol. November 1976.

The Beach Boys Love You. The Beach Boys. Brother-Reprise. April 1977. A strange record that is also the last consistently interesting Beach Boys release.

Pacific Ocean Blue. Dennis Wilson. Caribou. September 1977.

M.I.U. Album. The Beach Boys. Reprise. September 1978

L.A. (Light Album). The Beach Boys. Caribou. March 1979.

Keepin' the Summer Alive. The Beach Boys. Caribou. March 1980.

Carl Wilson. Carl Wilson. Caribou. March 1981.

Looking Back with Love. Mike Love. Boardwalk. October 1981.

Youngblood. Carl Wilson. Caribou. February 1983.

The Beach Boys. The Beach Boys. Caribou. 1985.

Brian Wilson. Brian Wilson. Sire. August 1988.

Summer in Paradise. The Beach Boys. Brother Entertainment. August 1992.

Good Vibrations: Thirty Years of the Beach Boys. The Beach Boys. Capitol. July 1993. A great boxed set if you can find it.

I Just Wasn't Made for These Times. Brian Wilson. MCA. August 1995.

Orange Crate Art. Brian Wilson and Van Dyck Parks. Warner Brothers. November 1995.

The Wilsons. Brian, Carnie, and Wendy Wilson. Mercury. September 1997.

Imagination. Brian Wilson. Giant. June 1998.

Live at the Roxy Theatre. Brian Wilson. BriMel. July 2000.

Live in Las Vegas. Al Jardine's Family and Friends. HV. September 2001.

Brian Wilson Presents Pet Sounds Live. Brian Wilson. BriMel. June 2002.

Mind If We Make Love to You. Wondermints. Smile Records. September 2002.

Sounds of Summer. The Beach Boys. Capitol. June 2003. This
   compilation in various lengths has sold and sold and sold and sold.
Gettin' in Over My Head. Brian Wilson. BriMel. June 2004.
Brian Wilson Presents Smile. Brian Wilson. Nonesuch. September
   2004. Unexpected, completed, a unique pop event.
What I Really Want for Christmas. Brian Wilson. Nonesuch. October
   2005.
That Lucky Old Sun. Brian Wilson. Capitol. August 2008.
A Postcard from California. Al Jardine. Robo Records. June 2010.
Brian Wilson Reimagines Gershwin. Brian Wilson. Disney. August 2010.
In the Key of Disney. Brian Wilson. Disney. October 2011.
Smile: The Beach Boys. The Beach Boys. Capitol. October 2011. The old
   tapes are arranged along the pattern set by the 2004 Brian Wilson
   recording, if you prefer everybody singing when they were young.
   Has some gaps.
That's Why God Made the Radio. The Beach Boys. Capitol. June. 2011.
   The 50th anniversary reunion CD has some filler as well as some
   masterful Brian Wilson "driving into the sunset" songs.
Music from Love and Mercy. Atticus Ross and Brian Wilson. Capitol.
   August 2015. Stands on its own as an interesting combination of
   soundtrack EDMish Beach Boys mash-up and straight old and
   new songs.
Beach Boys' Party! Uncovered and Unplugged. The Beach Boys. Capitol.
   November 2015.
The Beach Boys 1967: Sunshine Tomorrow. The Beach Boys. Capitol.
   June 2017.
Playback: The Brian Wilson Anthology. Brian Wilson. Rhino. September
   2017.
Unleash the Love. Mike Love. BMG. November 2017.

A CHRONOLOGICAL LISTING OF DVDS MENTIONED IN THE BOOK

....

Listed here are DVDs of movies in the order they first appeared in public, not when they were released as DVDs, to provide historical context: director if available, title, DVD company, year originally released.

Price, Will. *Allen Freed in Rock, Rock, Rock!* Alpha Home Entertainment, 1955.

Brown, Bruce. *Slippery When Wet.* Bruce Brown Films, 1958.

———. *Surf Crazy.* Bruce Brown Films, 1959.

———. *Barefoot Adventure.* Bruce Brown Films, 1960.

———. *Slippery When Wet.* Bruce Brown Films, 1960.

———. *Surfing Hollow Days.* Bruce Brown Films, 1961.

———. *Waterlogged.* Bruce Brown Films, 1962.

Usher, Gary. *One Man's Challenge.* Video Beat, 1962.

Taylor, Don. *Ride the Wild Surf.* Columbia Pictures, 1964.

Weinrib, Lennie. *Beach Ball.* Video Beat, 1965.

Rafkin, Alan. *Ski Party.* MGM Home Entertainment, 1965.

Witney, William. *The Girls on the Beach.* Video Beat, 1965.

Brown, Bruce. *The Endless Summer.* Bruce Brown Films, 1966. Deserves the term classic, worth watching.

Freeman, Jim, and Greg MacGillivray. *Five Summer Stories.* Action Sports Video, 1972.

Milius, John. *Big Wednesday.* Warner Brothers, 1978.

Leo, Malcolm. *The Beach Boys: An American Band*. Artisan Home
    Entertainment, 1985.

Smitzer, Michael. *Summer Dreams: The Story of the Beach Boys*.
    Fremantle Media, 1989.

Brown, Bruce. *The Endless Summer II*. Bruce Brown Films, 1994.

Arkush, Alan. *The Temptations*. Artisan Home Entertainment, 1998.

Brown, Bruce. *The Endless Summer Revisited*. Bruce Brown Films,
    2000.

Bleckner, Jeff. *The Beach Boys: An American Family*. Video Beat, 2000.

Gowers, Bruce. *An All-Star Tribute to Brian Wilson*. Radio City
    Entertainment, 2001.

Anderson, John. *Brian Wilson on Tour*. BriMel, 2002.

———. *Brian Wilson Presents Pet Sounds Live in London*. BriMel, 2002.

Brown, Dana. *Step into Liquid*. Lions Gate, 2003.

Noel, Chris. *Blonde Bombshell: The Incredible True Story of Chris Noel*.
    DVD Video, 2004.

Lena, Hank. *Musicares Presents a Tribute to Brian Wilson*. Eagle Vision,
    2004.

Leaf, David. *Beautiful Dreamer: Brian Wilson and the Story of Smile*.
    Rhino Home Video, 2005.

Hinsche, Billy. *Carl Wilson: Here and Now*. MFM Productions, 2011.

Pohlad, Bill. *Love and Mercy*. Lions Gate, 2015.

BIBLIOGRAPHY

....

Abbott, Kingsly. *Back to the Beach: A Brian Wilson and Beach Boys Reader*. London: Helter Skelter, 2003.

Badman, Keith. *The Beach Boys: The Definitive Diary of America's Greatest Band on Stage and in the Studio*. San Francisco: Backbeat Books, 2004.

Bai, Matt. *All the Truth Is Out: The Week Politics Went Tabloid*. New York: Knopf, 2014.

Burt, Rob. *Surf City, Drag City*. New York: Blandford, 1986.

Carlin, Peter Ames. *Catch A Wave: The Rise, Fall and Redemption of the Beach Boys' Brian Wilson*. New York: Rodale, 2006.

Christgau, Robert. *Any Old Way You Choose It: Rock and Other Pop Music, 1967–1973*. Baltimore: Penguin, 1973.

Cox, Harvey. *Fire from Heaven*. New York: Addison-Wesley, 1995.

Crowley, Kent. *Long Promised Road: Carl Wilson, Soul of the Beach Boys*. London: Jawbone Press, 2015.

Dallek, Matthew. *The Right Moment: Ronald Reagan's First Victory and the Decisive Turning Point in American Politics*. New York: Oxford University Press, 2004.

Di Perna, Alan, and Brad Tolinski. *Play It Loud: An Epic History of the Style, Sound, and Revolution of the Electric Guitar*. New York: Doubleday, 2016.

Doe, Andrew, and John Tobler, *Brian Wilson and the Beach Boys: The Complete Guide to Their Music*. London: Omnibus, 2004.

Donohue, H. E. F. *Conversations with Nelson Algren*. New York: Hill and Wang, 1963.

Elliott, Brad, *Surf's Up! The Beach Boys On Record, 1961–1981*. Ann Arbor: Pierian Press, 1982.

Gaines, Stephen. *Heroes and Villains: The True Story of the Beach Boys*. New York: Da Capo, 1995. First published by Dutton/Signet in 1986.

George, Nelson. *Where Did Our Love Go? The Rise and Fall of the Motown Sound*. New York: St. Martin's, 1985.

Goddard, Stephen B. *Getting There*. Chicago: University of Chicago Press, 1994.

Goldstein, Richard. *Another Little Piece of My Heart: My Life of Rock and Revolution in the '60s*. London: Bloomsbury Circus, 2015.

Granata, Charles L. *Wouldn't It Be Nice: Brian Wilson and the Making of the Beach Boys' Pet Sounds*. Chicago: Chicago Review Press, 2003.

Guralnik, Peter. *Last Train to Memphis: The Rise of Elvis Presley*. Boston: Little, Brown, 1994.

Horning, Susan Schmidt. *Chasing Sound: Technology, Culture and the Art of Studio Recording from Edison to the LP*. Baltimore: Johns Hopkins University Press, 2013.

Jacobs, Meg. *Panic at the Pump: The Energy Crisis and the Transformation of American Politics in the 1970s*. New York: Hill and Wang, 2016.

Katz, Mark. *Capturing Sound: How Technology Has Changed Music*. Berkeley: University of California Press, 2004.

Lambert, Phillip. *Inside the Music of Brian Wilson*. New York: Continuum, 2007.

Leaf, David. *The Beach Boys and the California Myth*. New York: Grosset and Dunlap, 1978.

Love, Mike. *Good Vibrations: My Life as a Beach Boy*. New York: Blue Rider Press, 2016.

Madley, Benjamin. *An American Genocide: The United States and the California Indian Catastrophe*. New Haven: Yale University Press, 2017.

Marcus, Greil. *Mystery Train: Images of America in Rock 'n' Roll Music*. New York: E. P. Dutton, 1975.

Marsh, David, and John Swenson. *The Rolling Stone Record Guide*. New York: Random House, 1979.

———. *The New Rolling Stone Record Guide*. New York: Random House, 1983.

McKeen, William. *Everybody Had an Ocean: Music and Mayhem in 1960s Los Angeles*. Chicago: Chicago Review Press, 2017.

McPartland, Stephen J. *Surf Beat: The Dick Dale Story*. North Strathfield, AU: C Music, 2000.

———. *Jan and Dean in Perspective, 1958–1968: The Grand High Potentates of California Rock*. North Strathfield, AU: C Music, 2004.

Moorefield, Virgil. *The Producer as Composer: Shaping the Sounds of Popular Music*. Cambridge, MA: MIT Press, 2010.

Noel, Chris. *Matter of Survival: The "War" Jane Never Saw*. Boston: Branden, 1987.

Nolan, Tom. "The Beach Boys: A California Saga." *Rolling Stone 94*, October 28, 1971; *Rolling Stone 95*, November 11, 1971.

Parissien, Steven. *The Life of the Automobile*. New York: St. Martin's, 2013.

Passmore, Mark Thomas. *Dead Man's Curve and Back: The Jan and Dean Story*. Bloomington, IN: 1st Books Library, 2003.

Priore, Domenic. *Smile: The Story of Brian Wilson's Lost Masterpiece*. London: Sanctuary Press, 2005.

Rothstein, Richard. *The Color of Law: A Forgotten History of How Our Government Segregated America*. New York: W. W. Norton, 2017.

Rusten, Ian, and Jon Stebbins. *The Beach Boys in Concert*. Milwaukee: Backbeat Books, 2013.

Sanders, Cheryl J. *Saints in Exile*. New York: Oxford University Press, 1996.

Sennett, Richard, with Jonathan Cobb. *The Hidden Injuries of Class*. New York: Knopf, 1973.

Sheffield, Rob. *Dreaming the Beatles*. New York: Dey Street, 2017.

Shiner, Lewis. *Glimpses*. New York: St. Martin's Griffin, 2001.

Slutsky, Allen. "Dr. Licks." In *Standing in the Shadows of Motown: The Life and Music of Legendary Bassist James Jamerson*. Wynnewood, PA: Dr. Licks Publishing, 1989.

Spofford, Tim. *Lynch Street: The May 1970 Slayings at Jackson State College*. Kent, OH: Kent State University Press, 1988.

Swift, Earl. *The Big Roads*. New York: Mariner Books, 2011.

Taves, Ann. *Fits, Trances, and Visions: Experiencing Religion and Explaining Experience from Wesley to James*. Princeton: Princeton University Press, 1999.

Tharp, Twyla. *Push Comes to Shove*. New York: Bantam Books, 1992.

Thompson, Ahmir. "Questlove." In *Mo' Meta Blues: The World According to Questlove*, by Ahmir Thompson and Ben Greenman, 41–42. New York: Grand Central, 2013.

Torrence, Dean. *Surf City: The Jan and Dean Story*. New York: Select Books, 2016.

White, Forrest. *The Fender Inside Story*. San Francisco: Backbeat Books, 1994.

White, Timothy. *The Nearest Faraway Place: Brian Wilson, the Beach Boys, and the Southern California Experience*. New York: Henry Holt, Owl Books, 1996.

Williams, Paul. *Brian Wilson and the Beach Boys: How Deep Is the Ocean?* New York: Omnibus, 1997.

Wilson, Brian, with Todd Gold. *Wouldn't It Be Nice: My Own Story*. New York: Harper Collins, 1991.

Wilson, Brian, with Ben Greenman. *I Am Brian Wilson: A Memoir*. Boston: Da Capo, 2016.